A brief account of the life of Howell Harris, Esq; extracted from papers written by himself. To which is added a concise collection of his letters from the year 1738, to 1772.

Howell Harris

ECCO
PRINT EDITIONS

A brief account of the life of Howell Harris, Esq; extracted from papers written by himself. To which is added a concise collection of his letters from the year 1738, to 1772.

Harris, Howell
ESTCID: T145179
Reproduction from British Library
The preface signed: B----** T----.
Trevecka : printed in the year, 1791.
103,[6],106-224p. ; 8°

Eighteenth Century
Collections Online
Print Editions

Gale ECCO Print Editions

Relive history with *Eighteenth Century Collections Online*, now available in print for the independent historian and collector. This series includes the most significant English-language and foreign-language works printed in Great Britain during the eighteenth century, and is organized in seven different subject areas including literature and language; medicine, science, and technology; and religion and philosophy. The collection also includes thousands of important works from the Americas.

The eighteenth century has been called "The Age of Enlightenment." It was a period of rapid advance in print culture and publishing, in world exploration, and in the rapid growth of science and technology – all of which had a profound impact on the political and cultural landscape. At the end of the century the American Revolution, French Revolution and Industrial Revolution, perhaps three of the most significant events in modern history, set in motion developments that eventually dominated world political, economic, and social life.

In a groundbreaking effort, Gale initiated a revolution of its own: digitization of epic proportions to preserve these invaluable works in the largest online archive of its kind. Contributions from major world libraries constitute over 175,000 original printed works. Scanned images of the actual pages, rather than transcriptions, recreate the works *as they first appeared.*

Now for the first time, these high-quality digital scans of original works are available via print-on-demand, making them readily accessible to libraries, students, independent scholars, and readers of all ages.

For our initial release we have created seven robust collections to form one the world's most comprehensive catalogs of 18th century works.

Initial Gale ECCO Print Editions collections include:

History and Geography
Rich in titles on English life and social history, this collection spans the world as it was known to eighteenth-century historians and explorers. Titles include a wealth of travel accounts and diaries, histories of nations from throughout the world, and maps and charts of a world that was still being discovered. Students of the War of American Independence will find fascinating accounts from the British side of conflict.

Social Science

Delve into what it was like to live during the eighteenth century by reading the first-hand accounts of everyday people, including city dwellers and farmers, businessmen and bankers, artisans and merchants, artists and their patrons, politicians and their constituents. Original texts make the American, French, and Industrial revolutions vividly contemporary.

Medicine, Science and Technology

Medical theory and practice of the 1700s developed rapidly, as is evidenced by the extensive collection, which includes descriptions of diseases, their conditions, and treatments. Books on science and technology, agriculture, military technology, natural philosophy, even cookbooks, are all contained here.

Literature and Language

Western literary study flows out of eighteenth-century works by Alexander Pope, Daniel Defoe, Henry Fielding, Frances Burney, Denis Diderot, Johann Gottfried Herder, Johann Wolfgang von Goethe, and others. Experience the birth of the modern novel, or compare the development of language using dictionaries and grammar discourses.

Religion and Philosophy

The Age of Enlightenment profoundly enriched religious and philosophical understanding and continues to influence present-day thinking. Works collected here include masterpieces by David Hume, Immanuel Kant, and Jean-Jacques Rousseau, as well as religious sermons and moral debates on the issues of the day, such as the slave trade. The Age of Reason saw conflict between Protestantism and Catholicism transformed into one between faith and logic -- a debate that continues in the twenty-first century.

Law and Reference

This collection reveals the history of English common law and Empire law in a vastly changing world of British expansion. Dominating the legal field is the *Commentaries of the Law of England* by Sir William Blackstone, which first appeared in 1765. Reference works such as almanacs and catalogues continue to educate us by revealing the day-to-day workings of society.

Fine Arts

The eighteenth-century fascination with Greek and Roman antiquity followed the systematic excavation of the ruins at Pompeii and Herculaneum in southern Italy; and after 1750 a neoclassical style dominated all artistic fields. The titles here trace developments in mostly English-language works on painting, sculpture, architecture, music, theater, and other disciplines. Instructional works on musical instruments, catalogs of art objects, comic operas, and more are also included.

The BiblioLife Network

This project was made possible in part by the BiblioLife Network (BLN), a project aimed at addressing some of the huge challenges facing book preservationists around the world. The BLN includes libraries, library networks, archives, subject matter experts, online communities and library service providers. We believe every book ever published should be available as a high-quality print reproduction; printed on-demand anywhere in the world. This insures the ongoing accessibility of the content and helps generate sustainable revenue for the libraries and organizations that work to preserve these important materials.

The following book is in the "public domain" and represents an authentic reproduction of the text as printed by the original publisher. While we have attempted to accurately maintain the integrity of the original work, there are sometimes problems with the original work or the micro-film from which the books were digitized. This can result in minor errors in reproduction. Possible imperfections include missing and blurred pages, poor pictures, markings and other reproduction issues beyond our control. Because this work is culturally important, we have made it available as part of our commitment to protecting, preserving, and promoting the world's literature.

GUIDE TO FOLD-OUTS MAPS and OVERSIZED IMAGES

The book you are reading was digitized from microfilm captured over the past thirty to forty years. Years after the creation of the original microfilm, the book was converted to digital files and made available in an online database.

In an online database, page images do not need to conform to the size restrictions found in a printed book. When converting these images back into a printed bound book, the page sizes are standardized in ways that maintain the detail of the original. For large images, such as fold-out maps, the original page image is split into two or more pages

Guidelines used to determine how to split the page image follows:

• Some images are split vertically; large images require vertical and horizontal splits.
• For horizontal splits, the content is split left to right.
• For vertical splits, the content is split from top to bottom.
• For both vertical and horizontal splits, the image is processed from top left to bottom right.

A

BRIEF ACCOUNT

OF THE

L I F E

OF

HOWELL HARRIS, Esq;

Extracted

FROM PAPERS WRITTEN BY HIMSELF.

To which is added

A concise Collection of his Letters

from the Year 1738, to 1772.

Dan. xii. 3.

And they that be wise shall shine as the brightness of the firmament; and they that turn many to righteousness, as the stars for ever and ever.

TREVECKA:

PRINTED IN THE YEAR,

MDCCXCI.

THE

PREFACE.

IN giving the public some Account of the Life of a man of an extraordinary character, there is danger, of either saying too much, or too little, of either expofing much of his weaknefs, or rendering him an object of contempt to the ignorant. Had he no infirmities, he would not be a mere man, if we display too many of his excellencies, we render the whole account, given of him, fufpicious. It has been often found, that faithfulnefs and fimplicity, have abundantly fupplied the place of bright parts, and great penetration in the hiftorian, and a judicious and candid reader, will feaft upon the undifguifed relation, of the actions of an open, unpremeditated character, with much more pleafure, than the perufal of a life drawn up according to the rules of art, and with laboured criticifm.

THE Compilers of the life, of the late Mr. *Howell Harris*, have not attempted to decorate, what he has written of himfelf,

or

or to illuſtrate any circumſtances, by aſſigning occult cauſes of this, or the other, particular action, or event. They knew him many years, not only as friends who occaſionally converſed with him, and were diſtant ſpectators, but as parts of his family, who ſaw all his movements, by day and night ; who generally heard his firſt thought, upon every new ſubject, or propoſed plan ; and were witneſſes of the ſteps he took to accompliſh what he belieſed, to be right; and they frequently took a conſiderable ſhare in the execution. Though their eſteem for him grew with the opportunities they had, of diſcovering his principles and practice, yet they did not implicitly, follow his words, farther than they were perſuaded in their own minds ; and they were not blind to his weakneſſes. They received real internal benefit from their ſpecial acquaintance with him, and to this day, his memory is dear and valuable, to them : and they are ready to ſay, that " Though dead, he yet ſpeaketh to them ; as well as to many more, who were of his large family, at *Trevecka.*"

The Compilers, determined to deliver to the public, a ſhort ſketch of his life, in all ſimplicity, hoping that thoſe who poſſeſs knowledge, of the ways of GOD, may reap ſome benefit, from the peruſal, and learn, like Mr. *Harris*, to follow, in ſimplicity, the leading of the LORD's Spirit, in their own line of life. And therefore, it is delivered to the reader, in its homely, but intelligible dreſs. The reader muſt therefore attend to the matter, and not to the manner, if he intends, either to judge with candour, or to reap any advantage from it.

THEY

PREFACE.

THEY put the draught of this sketch, of Mr. *Harris*'s life, into the hands, of the writer of this Preface, for his revision, as they knew, he was acquainted with the man, and some times, visited his house and family, and that though he did not labour in the same field, yet, he honored his character and approved of the general aim, of his proceedings. After inspecting the copy, it seemed however, best to leave it as when first compiled, with a few verbal alterations, as it will appear, that the dialect is agreeable to the place, of Mr. *Harris*'s nativity and education, and with a very few alterations, of any other kind.

THO' the writer of the Preface, found himself disposed to write a kind of apology for Mr. *Harris*, yet he will not take up much of the readers time, with it. He met with the fate of most worthy men, who have stepped out of the common beaten path, endeavouring to march forth in the defence of truth, to reform mankind. For he has been defamed, and many things laid to his charge, which prejudiced some against him, for a time, not only such, who are always ready to believe calumnies, but of well meaning and worthy men. The writer of this, looked upon him once, by means of what he heard, as at least, a suspicious character, but upon close enquiry, he received such well authenticated information, as removed his doubts, and rendered him more valuable in his eyes, than Mr *Harris*, ever would have been, had he not been, in a measure, missled, by misrepresentations.

THE natural warmth, of every man, of Mr. *Harris*'s complexion, would, and must naturally produce something *eccen-*

tric,

tric, in the moſt ordinary walk, or ſtation of life; but when we conſider the extraordinary courſe he took, it is not to be wondered at, that there not only appeared, but that ſomething really was eccentric, in ſeveral parts of his conduct He believed, he was called by GOD, to the work in which he ſpent himſelf, and indeed, if we are to judge by the fruits, it muſt be owned, by thoſe who believe that GOD has a ſpecial influence upon, and has the direction of his ſervants, that he had that particular call, from GOD. He was ſtill a man, and liable to miſtakes, and ſome of his miſtakes aroſe, from his zeal to accompliſh ſpeedily, the work, to which he was called. His natural impetuoſity, made him at times forget, that he that believeth will not make haſte. But is it right, to expect more, from a man acting in ſuch a ſphere, in our days, than from thoſe who have been made inſtruments, in the hand of GOD, to the greateſt purpoſes, even ſuch as relate to the kingdom of GOD ? Was *Luther*, or *Calvin*, or any of our *Engliſh* Reformers, without ſome ſtrong marks of eccentricity ? and is it not evident, that even their very eccentricity, tended to the accompliſhment of the great work, to which they were appointed ? Had they formed an eccentric plan, knowing it to be ſuch, they would have been inexcuſable, but the neceſſity of the caſe and time, produced an unpremeditated conduct,—which to cold ſpectation appeared very eccentric, but which was in reality, all circumſtances conſidered, regular, and neceſſary for that period *Luther*, was a man of warm paſſions, and his natural temper, would have been productive of the greateſt injuries, to himſelf and others, had not God appropriated his warmth, and made it ſubſervient to the great purpoſes of the reformation. It ſeems that the ſame may juſtly be

ſaid

PREFACE.

said of Mr. *Harris*'s temper, in relation to the purpose, for which GOD prepared him.

Mr. *Harris*, was naturally of an open and choleric disposition, he was no politician, in the general, or vulgar acception of the word. He was undisguised, in his words and actions, impetuous in his proceedings, would flatter no man, nor give up a particle of what he was persuaded to be truth, to please his dearest and nearest friend. The grace of GOD made a great alteration in his temper, and notwithstanding his activity, he would often retire, and spend many hours alone, in prayer, and in making supplications for his own soul, and the souls of his people, &c. His zeal for the house (that is the work) of the LORD, might be said to eat him up He frequently neglected his health, and was indifferent to food, at the stated times, and even to sleep. He neither attended to heat, or cold, if called to do something, which he believed, to be the will of GOD. Such was his indefatigableness, in the work of the LORD, during the space of thirty-nine years. Seventeen of which he spent in travelling through *Wales*, and great part of *England*, preaching, and exhorting, in the high-ways and hedges, wakes and revels, &c and though he had much opposition and persecution, yet he was more than conqueror, through CHRIST, that loved him. The remainder of his life, he mostly spent at *Trevecka*, where he faithfully ministered, to a large family, collected to him there, by means of his ministry, in former years. It appears from his life, that the collecting of this family, was unintentional, and a candid infidel, who takes a view of that house, and considers its beginning, progress, its state at his death, and present condition, must say, that there was a particular hand of GOD in it.

THO'

PREFACE.

Tho' he himself had as much oppoſition as any, by the Rulers in the eſtabliſhed Church, he ſaw that theſe things, in ſome meaſure, forced ſome out of the Church, tho' others left it from various motives, which were leſs excuſable, yet he remained immoveable in his attachment to it, and was notwithſtanding far from bigotry. He loved and honored all who he believed they were children and ſervants of GOD, of every denomination. (The writer of this was an inſtance of it) And according to his full perſuaſion, on this head, he regulated every thing, in his large family, conformable to it.

Mr. *Harris*, was looked upon by ſome, as a deſigning, and ſelf-intereſted man, his life and death have proved the contrary. And if we are to judge of cauſes, by the effects, we ſhall find that his principles and practice, have produced no bad moral, civil, or religious Facts, but on the contrary, his doctrines have produced virtuous men, good fellow-citizens, good ſubjects, and devout members, of the eſtabliſhed Church.

It is hoped, that the following ſimple relation of his life, will be a bleſſing to ſome, in leading them to the Fountain of Salvation, in our LORD JESUS CHRIST.

Your Devoted and affectionate

Servant in the Goſpel,

B———— ** T————,

A
BRIEF ACCOUNT
OF THE
LIFE
OF
HOWELL HARRIS, Efq;

I WAS born at *Trevecka*, in the Parifh of *Talgarth*, in the County of *Brecon*, on *January* 23d. 1714. My Parents kept me at School till I was eighteen years old, I made a confiderable progrefs in Learning, my Father then dying, I was fo far difcouraged, as not to entertain any thoughts of appearing in the world in a public capacity, and therefore undertook to keep a country School having no ferious friends to converfe with, and being now without any reftraints upon me, I was foon carried away with the ftream of vanity, pride, and youthfull diverfions; which got the afcendant in my foul.

B

THE

-THE many ſerious thoughts and reflexions I. before uſed to be ſeized with, were now obliged to give way to my pleaſures, and yet, having always an habitual conviction in my heart, I was not eaſy.

My ſphere of acquaintance among my ſuperiors became larger, and I had promiſing views of preferment in the world; being intended for Holy Orders.

BUT while I was thus about entering more publicly on the ſtage of life, and while all my corruptions grew ſtronger and ſtronger in me, and many providences ſeemed to concur to raiſe me in this world; the LORD was pleaſed to glorify his free Grace in awakening me to a ſenſe of the miſerable ſtate I was, and had been in, tho' I knew it not.

ABOUT the one and twentieth year of my Age, on *March* 30th 1735. our Pariſh Miniſter was uſing arguments to prove the neceſſity of receiving the Sacrament, and in anſwering objections which people make againſt going to it, viz. *our being not fit, &c.* I reſolved to go to the LORD's Table the following Sunday, being *Eaſter-day.* And by his ſaying, " If " you are not fit to come to the LORD's Table, you " are not fit to come to Church, you are not fit " to live, nor fit to die," I was convinced, and reſolved to leave my outward vanities, for as yet, I knew and ſaw but very little of my inward corruption; and as a ſtep to prepare myſelf (as I thought it)

I

I was immediately in going home from Church reconciled to a neighbour I had some difference with; acknowledging my own fault, and forgiving his. But knowing nothing of the Wedding-garment, being yet an utter stranger to all inward Religion, and the misery of my state by nature; and consequently knowing nothing truly of the LORD JESUS, but only what I learned by reading, and in notions, I had advanced no farther than forming a resolution to lead a new life, tho' I knew not where to begin or what to do.

BUT however, I went to the LORD's Table on *Easter-day*, and by repeating the words in the Confession, " The remembrance of our sins is grievous " unto us, the burden of them is intolerable." I began to reflect within me, to search whether this was my case, and soon found my confession was only words, and could not find any inward grief at the remembrance of them, nor indeed was their burden a heavy load to me : I was then convinced it ought to be so, and finding it was not, I saw I was going to the LORD's Table with a lie in my mouth; this, and a sense of the solemnity of the Sacred feast struck me, so that I was much inclined to withdraw, till my mind was quieted, by having determined to lead a new life; and in that resolution I went to the Table, and received the Pledge of GOD's dying love. Then I began that following week, and the week succeeding, to be more serious and thoughtful, and

was

was given to prayer, and ftrove to keep my heart and thoughts fixed on the LORD, but all in vain; thus I went on for a fortnight, till I had almoft loft my convictions.

WHEN on *April* the 20th, providence put a Book in my hand, I looked on the latter part of it, as a help to felf-examination, as foon as I began to read it, I was convinced, that in every branch of my Duty to GOD, to myfelf, and to my neighbours, I was guilty, and had fallen fhort. I found again the fame evening a Book written by *Bryan Duppa*, on the Commandments, which made my convictions fomewhat deeper; the more I read, the greater did the fpiritual light fhone in my mind, by fhewing me the extent of the Law of GOD, call-ing me to account, not only for outward grofs fins, but for our looks, aims, and ends, in all we think, fay, or do; then I faw plainly and clearly, that if I was to be judged by that Law, I was undone forever.

THUS the more I fearched into the nature of things, the more I faw myfelf, and all others, that I converfed with, in the broad way to deftruction. Then I was foon convinced, that I was void of all fpiritual life; and came to find I was carnal, and fold under fin; and felt I could no more believe, or mourn for my fins, than I could afcend to heaven. I began to humble myfelf by fafting, and denying myfelf in every outward comfort, but knew as yet

nothing

nothing of the inward self-denial which our SAVIOUR enjoins ; I had no knowledge of the Blood of JESUS, the only *Fountain opened for fin and for uncleanness,* Zec. xiii 1. and being a total ftranger to the life of faith , and therefore all this while in a damnable ftate, and in danger of final deftruction.

THUS having laid no foundation, I knew not the SAVIOUR's voice, till one day in prayer, I felt a ftrong impreffion on my mind to give myfelf to GOD as I was, and to leave all to follow him. But prefently felt a ftrong oppofition to it, backed with reafons, that if I would give myfelf to the LORD, I fhould lofe my liberty, and would then be not my own, or in my own power ; but after a great conflict for fome time, I was made willing to bid adieu to all things temporal, and chofe the LORD for my portion. I believe, I was then effectually called to be a follower of the LAMB, and had fome inward fatisfaction in my foul ; but had no evidence of my acceptance with GOD, till the following *Whitfunday,* at the Sacrament.

MAY 25th, 1735. I went thither, labouring and heavy laden under the guilt and power of my fins ; having read in a book, that if we would go to the Sacrament, fimply believing in the LORD JESUS CHRIST, we fhould receive forgiveness of all our fins, and fo it was to me : I was convinced by the HOLY GHOST, that CHRIST dyed for me, and that

all

all my fins were laid on him; I was now acquitted
at the bar of Juftice, and in my confcience, this
evidenced itfelf to be true faith, by the peace, joy,
watchfulnefs, hatred to fin, and fear of offending
GOD, that followed it —

I was then delivered from a grievous temptation,
that had followed me ever fince I had firft given myfelf to the LORD before that time I never knew what
inward trials, and fpiritual conflicts were, only now
and then I had fome uneafinefs from an awakened
confcience, which was quite different from thofe
fore trials that I bore from Atheiftical thoughts, that
made my life a burden to me; for they came with
fuch force and power on my mind, that I could not
withftand them. But at the Sacrament, by viewing
my GOD on the crofs, I was delivered from thefe
temptations; now, the world and all thoughts of
human applaufe and preferment were quite vanifh-
ed from my fight; the fpiritual world, and eternity
began (though as yet but faintly) to appear; now I
began to have other views and motives, different
from what I had; *viz.* I felt fome infatiable defires
after the falvation of poor finners; my heart longed
for their being convinced of their fins and mifery.
I alfo found myfelf a ftranger here; all my heart was
drawn from the world and vifible things, and were
in purfuit of a more valuable riches; I now began
to be more happy, and could not help telling in
going home from Church, that *Whitfunday*, that I

knew

knew my fins were forgiven me; though I had never heard any one make that confeffion before, or fay it could be obtained, but I was fo deeply convinced, that nothing could fhake my affurance of it. However I knew not whether I fhould continue in that ftate; having never converfed with any that had his face towards Sion, and who could inftruct me in the way of the LORD; but the cry of my foul being then, " Now or never; If GOD leaves thee now, and " thou ftifleft thefe convictions and bleffings, thou art " undone forever." This fear of loofing what I had then, kept me fafting, praying, and watching continually. Though I had peace with GOD; yet I was apprehenfive of feeing any of my old companions, left I fhould grow cold again; and this alfo induced me to keep clofe to him in all duties, and to keep a ftrict watch over my fpirit, heart, and lips, dreading all lightnefs of mind, and idle words, and foolifh jefting, which I was fo prone to by nature.

JUNE 18th, 1735. being in fecret prayer, I felt fuddenly my heart melting within me like wax before the fire with love to GOD my SAVIOUR, and alfo felt not only love, peace, &c. *but longing to be diffolved, and to be with* CHRIST; then was a cry in my inmoft foul, which I was totally unaquainted with before, *Abba Father! Abba Father!* I could not help calling GOD my FATHER; I knew that I was his child, and that HE loved me, and heard me. My foul being filled and

fatiated,

fatiated, crying, " 'Tis enough, I am fatisfied. Give
" me ftrength, and I will follow thee through fire and
" water —" I could fay I was happy indeed !—
There was in me *a well of water, fpringing up to
everlafling life* — John iv. 14. *The love of* God *was
fhed abroad in my heart by the* Holy Ghost.
Rom. v. 5.

Being ftill ignorant of God's method of bringing the loft fons of Adam home to himfelf, I did not
know in Scripture term, what I had now received ;
neither did I long retain this immediate fruition of
God by his Spirit ; but as I ftill kept fchool (waiting for my call from fome near relation to go to
Oxford) I felt fome rifings of anger in my heart
towards one of the children ; the enemy immediately accufed me, and alledged to me that I had now
forfeited all the happinefs, which I had juft before
enjoyed ; and that I was fallen from Grace, and
therefore in a worfe condition than ever ; this gave
me no fmall pain and confufion, and whilft I was in
this agony (hateing myfelf entirely for finning againft
this good God, the Saviour of finners) on account
of the lofs of that felicity I had enjoyed, I was ready
to defpond, but God pitied me, and foon fent that
word home to my foul, I change not. Mal.
iii. 6. That fuch word was fcriptural I knew not,
and how to apply it to myfelf was at a great lofs,
till light broke in upon my foul, to fhew me that my
falvation did not depend on my own faithfulnefs,

but

but on the faithfulnefs of JESUS CHRIST ; therefore, though I change, yet becaufe He changeth not, I was fecure. Then I was entirely freed from all fears, and found uninterrupted reft in the love and faithful-nefs of GOD my SAVIOUR.

I was all this while a total ftranger to all the con-troverfies about Religion, I only knew this, that GOD loved me, and would love me for his own name's fake freely to the end ; this made me to love him again, and ftudy how to fhew my love to him. I cannot exprefs the comfort I now enjoyed in my foul, being continually favoured with the Divine prefence, having my converfation in heaven. Now I could talk of nothing but fpiritual things, which foon brought contempt upon me : I was daily derid-ed by fome, and pitied by others ; fome ftrove to ter-rify me, and others to allure me with counfel, that favoured too much of the wifdom of this world, to have any weight with me. All my ftudy was now to fhew my gratitude to my GOD. But it grived me ftill, that I had neither feen nor heard of any in the country who feemed in earneft to *work out his own Salvation*, or to have any faving know-ledge of GOD in CHRIST, though I did not fo much then as imagine that I fhould be ufeful, fee-ing not the leaft probability of it, but rather the con-trary.

I had frequent thoughts of hiding myfelf from
C   my

my friends, dreading nothing more than to be known in the world.

THIS made me actually to drop my acquaintance with all ranks of people, and to reject offers that were made to raise my fortune in the world. I fold what I had, and gave it to the poor, and among the rest, such clothes as I thought too gay for a Christian. I saw by reading *Mat.* xix. 29. how dreadful it was, not to take GOD at his word, and then I had power to rely entirely on his word ; *And every one that hath forsaken houses, or brethren, or sisters, or father, or mother, or wife, or children, or lands for my name's sake, shall receive an hundred-fold, and shall inherit everlasting life.* Upon this promise I resigned my body and soul to his care forever.

FROM that time to the present, I can say that my life had been a life of faith, pleading with him, that I wholly depended on his blessed promises — I daily find him to be faithful, and they that trust in him shall not be ashamed. But this appears as Enthusiasm to flesh and blood, tho' we call GOD our FATHER, own him to be the disposer of all things, and that his word is truth ; yet we will not give him that credit, which we give to mortal unfaithful man : This indeed appears dreadful to me, and therefore I was determined to trust forever on his blessed promise for my temporal blessings, as it is all my trust for eternal life. Thus in all my wants, I had no where to

apply

apply but to the promife, and in that alone, I muſt declare, I have found enough.

In this light I ſaw my own miſery by nature, and confequently could not help feeing all that I had been acquainted with, of every rank and degree, going alfo as I had done in the *broad way that leads to diſtruction*. It very evidently appears by the teſtimony of God's word, and the conduct of the people, that this was the cafe then.

There being at that time a general ſlumber over the land — The generality of people ſpent the Lord's day contrary to the Laws of God and man; it being by none rightly obſerved , ——— neither had any one, whom I knew, the true knowledge of that God whom we pretended to worſhip. No fooner was the worſhip over, on the Lord's day, than the conduct of the people diſcovered that the heart was entirely alienated from all that was good. The remaining part of the day was ſpent in indulging the prevailing corruptions of nature ; all family worſhip being utterly laid afide (except among fome of the *Diſſenters*) while an univerfal deluge of ſwearing, lying, reviling, drunkennefs, fighting, and gaming had over-ſpread the country, like a mighty torrent , and that without any notice taken of, or a ſtop, as far as I had feen, been attempted to be put to it.

Seeing thus, rich and poor going as if it were
hand

hand in hand in the broad way to ruin; my foul was ftirred up within me; the Minifters were the firft that lay on my heart, I faw they were not in earneft, and did not appear to have any fenfe of their own danger, nor any feeling fenfe of the love of CHRIST; therefore, their inftructions delivered in fuch an unfeeling and indifferent manner, feemed to have no effect upon any of the hearers — I had never yet feen one man awakened by the preaching in the country — This view of their darknefs, deadnefs, and indifferency, made me out of the abundance of my heart, fpeak to fome of thofe with whom I was acquainted. But finding it had no effect, I took my felf to fecret prayer, and mourning, and engaged fome others to pray with me, and the LORD again renewed my ftrength.

THEN I could not help making it my Bufinefs to fpeak to all, I came near, of their danger: altho' I had but little knowledge of the way of falvation by faith, yet I was happy by feeling the bleffednefs of it in my own heart; fo that death and judgment were my principal fubjects of converfation, and the neceffity of praying and receiving the Sacrament, &c. I began to fet up family worfhip in my mother's houfe; and on Sunday morning fome of the neighbours would come to hear me reading the Leffons, and Plalms, &c. The evening I fpent with a few private friends, whom the LORD had now touched their

hearts

hearts with some sense of their danger. Now the fire of GOD did so burn in my soul, that I could not rest day nor night, without doing something for my GOD and SAVIOUR, nor could I go with satisfaction to sleep, if I had not done something for his glory that day. Time was so precious, that I knew not how to improve it entirely to the glory of GOD, and the good of others. When alone I was taken up wholly in reading, praying, or writing, &c. and also continued to go on exhorting the poor people, and they flocked to hear me every Sunday evening. I soon became the public talk of the country, but I was carried as on the wings through all my trials, both inward and outward — I was highly favoured, indeed, by the FRIEND of sinners! and was now quite another man; — I feared nothing, though my life was in danger from the threats of such as loved darkness rather than light; yet I was not moved, but went on comfortably, little thinking all this time, that I was at any time to be more public. Thus I spent that Summer. 1735.

IN the beginning of *November* following, I went to *Oxford*, and entered at *St. Mary's Hall*, under the tuition of Mr. *Hart*. But having now no taste for the entertainments there, I spent the greatest part of my time in secret prayers, or in the public worship. Now my friends were in hopes I should be effectually cured of my Enthusiasm; (as they called it) but

the

the LORD JESUS had now got poſſeſſion of my heart; ſo that notwithſtanding the promiſing proſpect before me, having had the promiſe to be admitted as Sub-Tutor at a great School, and a Benefice of 140*l per annum* by a certain Gentleman; and altho' I was encompaſſed with fair proſpects, yet when I ſaw the irregularities, and immoralities which ſurrounded me there, I became ſoon weary of the place, and cried to GOD to deliver me from thence, and thus, after keeping that term, I was again brought to my dear friends in *Wales.*

AFTER my return, I was occupied in going from houſe to houſe, until I had viſited the greateſt part of my native Pariſh, together with thoſe of neighbouring ones; the people now began to aſſemble by vaſt numbers, ſo that the houſes wherein we met, could not contain them. The word was attended with ſuch power, that many on the ſpot cried out to GOD for pardon of their ſins — and ſuch as lived in malice, confeſſed their ſins, making peace with each others, &c and appeared in concern about their eternal ſtate. Family worſhip was ſet up in many houſes, and the Churches, as far as I had gone, were crouded, and likewiſe the LORD's table.

IT was now high time for the enemy to make a ſtand in another manner, therefore he not only influenced the populace to revile, and perſecute me, but cauſed the Magiſtrates, and Clergy to beſtir them-

themſelves: the former to threaten me, and ſuch
as would receive me to their houſes, with fines, &c.
while the latter ſhewed their Indignation, and uſed
their endeavours to diſcourage me by other means,
&c. This put ſome ſtop, for a ſhort time, yet it
could not extinguiſh the flame that was kindled.
Though fear kept many back, yet ſuch as were
drawn by the divine attraction, could not be affright-
ed, and I continued ſtill to meet thoſe ſecretly, and
alſo the following ſpring I continued in going from
houſe to houſe as before, ſpeaking to all that were
inclined to hear me. By this time I gained acquaintance with ſeveral *Diſſenters*, who kindly received me to
their houſes. In this manner I went on, till adviſed
by a particular friend the latter end of the Summer, in 1736. to ſet up a School at *Trevecka*, which
I did, but removed from thence to the Pariſh
Church. By this means, great many young perſons had laid hold of this opportunity, and came to
be farther inſtructed in the way of Salvation, but Oh,
with a bleeding heart I now think of many of them,
ſeeing they were likely to end in the fleſh, after they
had begun well in the Spirit.

THE latter end of this year, a man went about
to inſtruct young people to ſing Pſalms, this gave
me another opportunity to ſhew my love to my dear
fellow ſinners, for the people being met to learn, and
to hear him ſing, there was no objection made, any
more than to aſſemblies met to Cock-fighting, danc-
ing,

ing, &c. I laid hold of this opportunity, when he had done teaching them to fing, I would give them a word of exhortation, and thereby many were brought under convictions, and many religious Societies were by thefe means formed. I began in imitation of the Societies which Dr. *Woodward* gave an account of, in a little Treatife he wrote on that head. There being as yet no other Societies of the kind in *England* or *Wales*. The *Englifh Methodifts* not being as yet heard of, tho' the LORD was now, as I found afterward, working on fome of them in *Oxford*, and elfewhere — But when I was thus expofed to all kinds of oppofition, tho' I faw no proper fteps which I could fecurely take ; yet the way was again opened, but was threatened that I fhould be filenced.

BUT however, the beginning of the following Summer, in 1737, a certain Gentleman in *Radnor-fhire* fent for me to difcourfe at his houfe, this ftirred the curiofity of fome of the better fort of people to come to hear me ; whilft others in converfing with me, had their prejudices much removed ; and others were convinced. I had reafon to believe the LORD would be pleafed to blefs my labours, though I ftill continued to teach School, yet I went out every night to fuch places where I was fent for, and did the fame on the Holy-days, and on the Sabbath — until, at laft, about the latter end of the year 1737, I was turned out of my School, which conduced to enlarge my fphere —

AFTER

AFTER this, I readily complied with every invitation, and went wherever I was fent for, by day and night; dicourfing generally three or four, and fometimes, five and fix times a day, to crowded auditories.

Now I was loaded with all manner of calumnies, from all quarters: the Magiftrates threatened me, the Clergy preached againft me, branding me with the character of a falfe prophet, and deceiver, &c. the Mob was active, laying in wait with intentions of mifchief, yet during all this I was carried, as on the wings of an Eagle, triumphantly above all— I took no particular Texts, but difcourfed freely as the LORD gave me utterance. The gift I had received was as yet to convince the confcience, of fin.

THERE appeared now, a general reformation in feveral counties —— Public diverfions became unfafhionable, and religion became the common talk; places of divine worfhip were every where crowded. The *Welch* Charity Schools began now to fpread, by the procurement of the Rev. Mr. *Griffith Jones,* of *Llanddouror*; and people in general expreffed their willingnefs to be litterally inftructed; and Societies were alfo fet up in many places.

ABOUT this time, I heard by a friend that came from *London*, of a young Clergyman, namely Mr. *Whitefield,* that preached four times a day; and was

much

much bleffed. In hearing this, my heart was united
to him in fuch a manner, that I never felt the like
connexion with any ore before, but yet I had not
the leaft profpect of ever feeing him ; being informed
that he had gone beyond Sea, it being his firft voyage
to *America*. But in the beginning of *January* 1738.
I was agreeably furprized by a Letter from him   he
having providentially heard of me, wrote to me in
order to encourage me to go on.   I was at this time
greatly diftreffed in refpect to my itinerary way of
preaching , yet I profecuted my work with the utmoft activity.

THUS I went on, having fweet fellowfhip with
GOD daily in private prayer, and at the Sacrament,
which I conftantly attended — Yet ft·ll being not
fully fettled as to my method of proceeding, I was
fhaken by Satan, and by a fenfe of the greatnefs of the
work, and of my own weaknefs and incapacity for
it , but ftill I was conftrained to go on, by the im-
portunity of the generality of the people, and by the
vifible good tendency of my labours, and the united
call and approbation of many whom I efteemed as
gracious Minifters, and by the continual power I felt
with me in the work.   Thus my fpirit was much
enlivened, efpecially when in the LORD's work, and
I feared neither nen nor devils.   Such power and
courage I had not by nature, therefore it appeared to
me to be undoubtedly fupernatural and from GOD.

As

As to the subject of my discourse, it was all given unto me in an extraordinary manner, without the least premeditation, it was not the fruit of my memory; for, naturally, my memory was bad, therefore it was the effect of the immediate strong impulse which I felt in my soul, I was not able to rest, consequently, necessity was laid on my spirit to go and awaken souls. Thus I went on, tho' with fear and trembling, lest others of bad intentions should take occasion to go about after my example; therefore I prayed that I might know GOD's will more perfectly, whether he was the only object of my love and desire, and whether his glory, and the salvation of my fellow sinners was the only objects of my view — And after examining the matter thus, I had power to rely, in all things, on the strength of the grace that is in CHRIST JESUS, for power to carry me through the great work, and that if his honor should call me to suffer, to be imprisoned and tortured, I should find him a faithful friend in every trial, in death, and to all eternity.

By this time the Rev. Mr. *Rowlands*, and some other young Clergymen were called in *Wales*, to preach the Gospel in the same extemporary manner as I was.

THUS, altho' I had many comfortable assurances, that my commission was from above, yet I was not thoroughly confirmed about it in my own heart, until

I was

I was fummoned to appear before a perfon of diftinction, to render an account of my going about in the manner I did, then thefe words were brought with power to my foul, from *Rev.* iii. 7, 8. *Behold, I have fet before thee an open door, and no man can fhut it, &c.* By the gracious effect this left on my foul, I am confirmed and perfuaded, it was applied to me by the HOLY GHOST.

My life being now in danger in feveral places by the Mob, efpecially in *Feb.* 1739. when they found I could not be profecuted as a Rioter, becaufe it did not appear I difturbed the peace; yet in *Montgomeryfhire*, a Knight, a Clergyman, and two Juftices, whilft I was difcourfing, came, attended by a Conftable, with the Mob, and took cognizance of me, and fuch as met together, to hear my exhortation in a place unlicenced; then they began to charge me with a breach of the Conventicle Act — I told the Magiftrate that I was a Conformift, and for that reafon, not fubject to the pennalties of that Statute; then they faid, we fhall confult the beft Lawyers in order to know if there is a Law to be enforced againft you; and if there is, that I fhould expect to fuffer its utmoft extremity — My perfecutors continued thus to threaten me until Seffion came on, at which time a Lawyer was confulted, and the cafe was dropped.

AFTER my difmiffion I went to *Merionethfhire*, where, I truft, the LORD bleffed the feed fown to ſome. In my return from thence, I came by *Dinas-Mowddwy*, and diſcourſed there; and at the requeſt of a friend, I went on to *Machynlleth*. But at my firſt entrance there, I found none were diſpoſed to receive me; however, I propoſed to preach the Goſpel to ſuch as met in the ſtreet, being placed in an open window or door in an upper room, but I was ſoon obliged to deſiſt, by the noiſe of the multitude, who continued hollowing, threatening, ſwearing, and flinging ſtones, or any thing they could lay their hands on — and eſpecially by an Attorney's coming up to me, with ſuch rage and fury in his looks, and his mouth ſo full of the language of hell, as if his name was *Legion*, and with him a Gentleman, and a Clergyman, in the ſame ſpirit and language, to head the Mob, &c. one of them diſcharged a Piſtol at me, I received no hurt, but was obliged to go among them into the ſtreet, not expecting that I ſhould eſcape alive, ſeeing every circumſtance threatening me with death ——— but my hour was not yet come; tho' they uſed me ill, yet I was miraculouſly preſerved: and at laſt one of the Mob was diſpoſed to fetch my horſe; and as ſoon as I mounted, they obſerved which way I went, and croſſed my road, and began again to throw ſticks and ſtones at me, till the LORD delivered me out of their hands.

By theſe means, and many other trials, which I often paſſed through, I was at length ſo accuſtomed to them, that when I aroſe in the morning, I was daily in expectation of my croſſes and trials. I be-

came

came more acquainted with the world and myself; and could atteſt by my own experience, the truth of that expreſſion, which at firſt ſeems harſh, viz. that, "Man is a mixture of beaſt and devil."

My natural ſtrength by this time, was ſo ſpent by inceſſant labours night and day, that frequently when I went before a congregation, I felt ſuch a bodily weakneſs, that I could hardly ſtand, until our SAVIOUR would enable me by faith to plead that promiſe in *Iſa.* xl. 31. *That they who wait upon the Lord ſhall renew their ſtrength, &c.* Then I preſently felt by faith, inſtantaneous ſtrength ſufficient for my ſoul and body, to carry me through my work; yea I felt it as really, as ever I have felt the benefit of food when hungry, or the warmth of fire when cold.

Thus I continued and went on ſtill through the Counties of *South Wales,* until I arrived at *Cardiff,* where I was much refreſhed by the ſight of Mr. *Whitefield* — this was the firſt time I met him to converſe face to face *.

ABOUT

* See Whitefield's Journal at Cardiff, March 7, and 8. 1739. where he gives the following account of Mr. Harris, viz ——

"After I came from the Seat, I was much refreſhed with the ſight of my dear Brother *Howell Harris,* whom, though I knew not in perſon, I have long ſince loved in the Bowels of JESUS CHRIST, and have often felt my ſoul drawn out in prayer in his behalf — A burning and ſhining light has he been in thoſe parts — a Barrier againſt prophaneneſs and immorality, and an indefatigable promoter of the true Goſpel of JESUS CHRIST.
About

ABOUT the end of *March*, 1739. I went to *London*, where I received farther Gospel light by conversing with a friend, who among other observations, said to this effect; "I see many people concerned about "working in themselves, &c. but few seem to be "con-

About three or four years, GOD has inclined him to go about doing good. He is now above Twenty five years of Age Twice he has applied (being every way qualified) for holy Orders, but was refused, under a false pretence, that he was not of age, though he was then Twenty two years and Six Months. About a Month ago he offered himself again, but was put off. Upon this, he was, and is still resolved to go on in his work, and indefatigable zeal has he shewn in his Master's service. For three years (as he told me from his own mouth) he has discoursed almost twice every day for three or four hours together, not authoritatively, as a Minister, but as a private person, exhorting his Christian Brethren He has been, I think, in seven Counties, and has made it his business to go to Wakes, &c to turn people from such lying vanities Many Alehouse-people, Fidlers, Harpers, &c (*Demetrius* like) sadly cry out against him, for spoiling their Business. He has been made the subject of numbers of Sermons, has been threatened with public prosecutions, and had Constables sent to apprehend him But GOD has blessed him with inflexible courage — Instantaneous strength has been communicated to him from above, and he still continues to go on from conquering to conquer. He is of a most Catholic spirit, loves all that loves our LORD JESUS CHRIST, and therefore he is stiled by Bigots, a *Dissenter* He is contemned by all that are lovers of pleasure more than lovers of GOD, but GOD has greatly blessed his pious endeavours Many call, and own him as their spiritual Father, and, I believe, would lay down their lives for his sake He discourses generally in a field, from a wall, a Table, but at other times in a house, or any thing else. He has established near thirty Societies in *South Wales*, and still his sphere of Action is enlarged daily. *He is full of faith, and the Holy Ghost* ——

WHEN

" convinced of the neceſſity of believing in CHRIST,
" before they can do any thing acceptable in his
" fight." There came ſuch a freſh light with theſe

WHEN I firſt ſaw him, my heart, was knit cloſely to him.
I wanted to catch ſome of his fire, and gave him the right
hand of fellowſhip with my whole heart After I had ſaluted
him, and given a warm exhortation to a great number of
people, who followed me to the Inn, we ſpent the remainder of
the evening in taking ſweet council together, and telling one
another what GOD had done for our ſouls. My heart was ſtill
drawn out towards him more and more A divine and ſtrong
ſympathy ſeemed to be between us, and I was reſolved to promote his intereſt with all my might. Accordingly we took an
account of the ſeveral Societies, and agreed on ſuch meaſures as
ſeemed moſt conduſive to promote the common intereſt of our
LORD. Bleſſed be GOD, there ſeems to be a noble ſpirit gone
out into *Wales*, and I believe e'er long, there will be more viſi-
ble fruits of it What inclines me ſtrongly to think ſo is, that
the Partition-wall of Bigotry and party-zeal is broken down,
and Miniſters and Teachers of different Communions, join with
one heart and one mind to carry on the kingdom of JESUS
CHRIST — The LORD make all the Chriſtian world thus minded For till this is done, I fear we muſt deſpair of any great
Reformation in the Church of GOD. After much comfortable
and encouraging diſcourſe with each other, we kneeled down
and prayed, and great enlargement of heart GOD was pleaſed to
give me in that duty.

THIS done, we ate a little ſupper, and then after ſinging a
Hymn, we went to bed, praiſing and bleſſing GOD, for bringing us face to face. I doubt not but Satan envied our happineſs. But I hope, by the help of GOD, we ſhall make his
kingdom ſhake *God loves to do great things by weak inſtru-*
ments, that the Power may be of God, and not of man. After
being much refreſhed by laſt night's reſt——about ten in the
morning, according to appointment, I went to the Town-hall,
and preached for about an hour and a half to a large aſſembly of
people. My dear Brother *Howell Harris* ſat cloſe by me——"

words

words to my heart, that I could not but infist that Faith is the fundamental Grace in the fpiritual work, and the genuine fpring of all our obedience : and till we receive this Grace, we cannot apprehend the righteoufnefs of CHRIST, and confequently cannot fay that we are juftified, &c. This frefh light, brought alfo with it frefh convictions, which funk deeper and deeper into my fpirit; efpecially by reading part of *Cotton, on the Covenant of Grace*; whilft he was fhewing how far one might go with right notions of Salvation, and yet not rightly believe, truft or rely confidently on the merits of CHRIST; but in fomewhat done by us, or in us : And when he fhewed the many falfe refts people are apt to acquiefce in fhort of CHRIST, viz. fome reft in their outward profeffion of the true religion; others becaufe they are Orthodox in their principles; and others becaufe they have reformed their lives, and do abound in all good works, &c. and whilft he fhewed all thefe were our works, and not the Blood of CHRIST, and a perfon building his hope here, was not building on CHRIST (although I had been brought from all thefe refts a long time before, by reading the *Sincere Convert*) I was wounded, by clofe re-examination; efpecially as he went on to fhew that we may truft in our faith, good frames, and performances, &c. (tho' they were good in their places, yet to rely on them is idolatry) and not on CHRIST's Blood only. And though I had the feed

E   fown

fown in my foul four years before, and had daily feel-
ings of GOD's love in my heart, yet the awakenings
that I felt this time made fo deep an impreffion on
my heart, that I could hardly bear them — yea, I can
fay that my fpirit was greatly diftreffed with deep
anguifh of foul for fome days together, until I was
refrefhed by that text in *Rev* xxii. 17. *Whofoever
will, let him take the water of life freely.* This fuf-
tained me, and I felt I was willing to let GOD do
what he pleafed with me.

BUT yet ftill, I was troubled with fome reafon-
ings, about going directly to CHRIST in every condition; till, at one time, a woman came to me to relate, how all the night fhe had been in diftrefs and
perplexity, reafoning with the enemy, whether fhe
was a child of GOD or not, and that fhe could have
no reft or fatisfaction, till it came to her mind to go
to CHRIST as fhe was, and that fhe had thereupon
peace, and victory — Upon hearing this, and fome
preaching afterwards, that people fhould come to
CHRIST as they are, without reafoning in themfelves,
I was made to ceafe from reafoning, and to go with
all my complaints, and fears, and lay them before the
FRIEND of finners, who loved me freely, and not
for any good in me. Now that legal principle of
fitting myfelf for CHRIST, and of being afraid to go
to him when I was not in a good frame were rooted
out of my heart; then I learned to look and go directly to CHRIST at all times, and in all circum-
ftances.

I

I parted this fummer with many dear friends in London, and came home to *Trevecka*. The next day I was called by bufinefs to *Abergavenny*; and was edified in reading *Bunyan's Law and Grace*, by the way: then my foul was much revived at the kind and hearty reception I had from fome of my dear friends there; I could not part with them till after nine at night, — then I went, and came home about one in the morning, —— notwithftanding I had travelled thefe eight days paft very hard, and had many Letters to write, and alfo was to difcourfe with fome of my neighbouring friends before noon, I was affifted to fit up all night, to read, write, and pray, yet the LORD enabled me to difcourfe with great ftrength of body at noon, and again in the evening, with much power, near the *Hay*, for about two hours. From thence I fet off about five miles farther; and to bed about twelve.

THE following day, as I was going to *Long-Town,* in *Herefordfhire*, many young people was crowding towards a feaft kept there; I had a fpirit of pity and tendernefs to them; and from that fpirit fpoke home to perfuade them from going; becaufe I had fome concern in my foul that GOD was fo publicly dif-honoured, and that fouls are in fuch a miferable con-dition, then I had fome drawings in my mind to go to the feaft, and I was made willing to fuffer whatever I fhould meet, and after having prayed alone, ven-

tured

tured to go thither in the name of G O D; and before
I came to the great crowd, I came to a few who
were together at their diverſion, to theſe I took occaſion to ſpeak, on account of one of them ſwearing,
and while I was ſpeaking with theſe, the news went
to the great crowd that I was there, and they ran
up by hundreds, till, I believe, there was in a little
time about two thouſand around me; and the LORD
gave me courage to attack the Devil in his own quarters — and made my face as a flint — ſupplying me
with proper matters; and eſpecially when I ſaw ſome
Gentlemen and Ladies coming up, I was made
ſtronger and ſtronger to humble their pride —— I
was alſo moved to apply home to the Miniſter of the
pariſh, and two Juſtices that were preſent, aſking
how they could give account of their ſtewardſhip,
while they countenanced pride, ſwearing, and drunk-
enneſs, &c. ſome of the Gentlemen laughed at me, and
one cried, " Take the Babbler down," but my time
was not yet come. I went from thence towards
Abergavenny, there the vileſt of the Town came to
hear me, and the LORD helped me to deliver my
meſſage faithfully, and boldly at Mr. *J——* Mr. *E.
Jones* was preſent: we went to bed about two o clock
in the morning.

HAVING now, by the ſtrength of the LORD, a
power and courage to reſiſt the Devil in two Towns,
I went on my way to the third, viz. *Pont-y-Pool*, and
thereafter I had been led to diſcourſe much about the

courage

courage of *Daniel, Shadrach, Meſhach,* and *Abednego,*
and how the LORD ſtands by his people in the day of
battle, &c. I was at laſt honoured with the fulfilment
thereof in myſelf — for Mr. *C*——*H*—— came
upon us, and did read the Riot-act, ordering us to
ſeparate in an hour's time; — At his firſt coming,
our ſpirits were a little diſcouraged, but immediately
the LORD ſtrengthened me to tell him, that in obedience to his Majeſty's order we would ſeparate;
then he ordered a Conſtable to take care of me; I
had full courage in the inward man to ſay, that I was
willing to go to priſon, and to death to ſave ſouls,
but that we had here no Riot, nor Sedition againſt
Church or State; and I aſked him if he read that Act
at Cock-matches, &c. but he continued his threaten-
ings that he would take notice of as many as he
could, and if they did not diſperſe as before, they
ſhould die without benefit of Clergy — The aſſembly
continued unmoved, and eaſy, I told him, we would
part, having firſt prayed for him, that the curſe of
thoſe people may not fall on his head, and that GOD
would not lay this to his charge in the day of judgment, where you ſhall ſtand not as a Juſtice of the
Peace, but as a reſponſible creature, to give an account how you did bear the ſword of Juſtice. he then
replied that, " That did not trouble him at preſent"—
Then we went to prayer, and when I begged GOD
would meet him, as he did *Saul,* with his ſaving grace,
&c. he went away, — and the people moſt of them
in tears, and ſo we parted in great love.

I was

I was fupported and more chearful than ufual all the time. Late in the evening I went with the Conftable, and a great number of people before him, and having confulted with fome friends (though it was my own inclination to go to prifon) I gave two bails to anfwer at the next great Seffion at *Monmouth*. Then I faid farther, that I was furprifed that Major *H——*'s fon, (for he was a good natured man, &c.) fhould be the firft perfecutor of a proteftant peaceable affembly; he faid, he had his orders from above—I afked him, Was it from heaven? And he faid, " No, I did not mean that," faid he: I told him that I thought, if his Majefty knew how loyal and harmlefs we were, that he would not love you the better for fuppreffing us — Thus I parted with him, having left fome arrows in his confcience, about his being foon to give an account of himfelf at a dreadful tribunal — but that I had, and would pray for him, and he thanked me.

THIS being about the middle of *June*, I was not to appear at the great Seffion in *Monmouth* till *Auguft* — Therefore, in the mean time, I was determined to be diligent in the work of my LORD; I went from hence to *Briftol*, where I had a fweet converfation with my friends there — Then I went to a Society of *Welfhmen*, where I expounded for near two hours. Thence to hear Mr. *John Wefley*, whom I had heard much talk of, and loved much from what I have heard of him; but had fome prejudice againft him,

him, becaufe he did not hold the Perfeverance of the Saints, and the doctrine of Election, &c. He preached on *Ifaiah* xlv. 22. *Look unto me, and be ye faved, all the ends of the earth. for I am God, and there is none elfe.* And fo excellently, and clearly, held forth free Juftification by faith, without the works of the Law — the neceffity, duty, and priviledge of every one's looking to JESUS for righteoufnefs, ftrength, and all, inftead of reafoning, &c. and the Spirit of GOD attended his difcourfe to my foul in fuch a manner, that much of the LORD's glory broke in upon my foul; and my prejudice againft him fell away — and I was convinced that he was a faithful Minifter of JESUS CHRIST —— efpecially when I went to him at Mrs. *G—*. where he was vaftly enlarged in prayer for me, for the Rev. Mr. *G. Jones*, and all *Wales*. Thus I believe, from the benefit I received, that my going to *Briftol* was from GOD.

HAVING parted with all friends at *Briftol*, I fet out for *Wales*; the door now opens wider and wider to the feveral Counties of *Glamorgan, Brecon, Carmarthen*, and part of *Radnor, Cardigan*, and *Pembrokfhire*. I had reafon to believe my labours were attended with much blefling.

THEN I returned from this round, and arrived at home in *Trevecka, Brecconfhire*, on the 7th of *Auguft*; and in the evening I went toward *Abergavenny* in my

way

way to *Monmouth* Affizes; and fpent the night at Mr. *J.* moft agreeably with fome Chriftian friends, whofe hearts the LORD has inclined to go with me, to bear a part in my fufferings, fhould occafion require.

THEN I went on to *Monmouth*; in the mean time hearing that my perfecutors were refolved to have me punifhed, to the utmoft rigour of the Law, whatever it might coft them. I knew that I had neither friends nor money to make any defence, or to help me that way; for I had renounced all my former friends, and if I was deluded, as they faid, and not fent of GOD, I knew that he would not ftand by me: But however, this being my cafe, it drove me to fend ftrong cries to the LORD, that he would give me a clearer proof of my commiffion, and whether I fuffered for his caufe, or for my own imprudence and indeliberatenefs, as fome faid I did. But the LORD comforted me foon, by that portion of Scripture, *Eſt.* VI. 9. *Thus fhall it be done to the man whom the King delighteth to honor;* yet then it appeared to me as a wrong ftep to honor, to be obliged to ftand at the Bar, to bear the contempt of the Court, and the whole County, not confidering that the Crofs is the way to the Crown, and that the reproach of CHRIST is the greateft honor!

WHEN I came to *Monmouth,* the LORD, though without my knowledge, had animated many friends,

and

and brought them from feveral parts, as *London*, *Gloucefter* and *Wales*, &c. to ftand by me . but the Magiftrates, after confulting about the affair, thought it not expedient to appear againft me , and fo I was difmiffed ——

AFTER my difmiffion, I was more eftablifhed in my own foul, that my Miffion was from GOD; efpecially as I had fo often applied for Holy Orders, and was rejected, for no other reafon but for my preaching as a Layman. I felt no fcruple ever fince, but have been more and more eftablifhed and confirmed, both from Scripture examples, and by the judgment and practice of the Church, and former Eminent Divines. As to the lawfulnefs of Laymen's preaching, in fome cafes, and at times of neceffity, I faw in the Acts of the Apoftles, the account of *Appollus* and others, who were fcattered by the death of *Stephen*, having no other Miffion than being moved by the HOLY GHOST, and love to the immortal fouls of their fellow creatures, — I thought a greater time of neceffity could hardly be than at prefent, when the whole Country, in a curfory fenfe, lay in a lukewarm, dead condition — in many Churches, for fome months together, there was no fermon; and in other places, an Englifh learned difcourfe to a Welfh illiterate congregation — and where an intelligible fermon was preached, it was fo legal, in the language of the old covenant, and advancing man's works, &c. not treating of a Mediator, that fhould any give heed to it,

F   they

they could eafily perceive that they were far from being lead thereby to CHRIST, the only new and living way to GOD.   Seeing this, and feeling the love of CHRIST in my heart, I faw an abfolute neceffity of going about to propagate the Gofpel of my dear MASTER and REDEEMER ——

HAVING parted with my friends, who came to ftand by me at *Monmouth* Seffion, I went on my way with fome friends, to *Llanvihangel-Cerrig-Cornel,* and offered to difcourfe there for my LORD and MASTER, but here I met much oppofition, being contradicted, ridiculed, and abufed, which I faw was given me as a thorn in the flefh, to humble me, leaft I fhould be exalted above meafure, but Satan, thou art chained! Thus having been much humbled in the inward man, I was enabled at laft to conquer fome of them by love and meeknefs, then I had quiet, and an open door to difcourfe and pray, &c. Surely times of trials are very fweet feafons, they draw forth our faith into exercife,—— and knit our hearts more clofely to GOD and his people.

THUS I went through the Counties of *South-wales* the fecond time this year, having new ftrength and a new commiffion from the LORD.   I was followed in general by thofe of the eftablifhed Chuich, becaufe I profeffed myfelf a Churchman, and that I had no intention to draw them from the Church. But when I began to fhew them the danger thoroughly,

oughly, and that the doctrine they hard was not of our Articles and Homilies, nor maintained by the old Reformers, &c. but that it was the Covenant of works in the whole, or in part, and that it was Morality, and not CHRIST that was preached almoft every where, &c. then I was looked upon as an enemy to the Church, tho' all this while, I was endeavouring to revive it — The *Diſſenters* at firſt liked me much, as I was encouraging the people to go any where to hear, where CHRIST was preacned, and where they found moſt benefit, and when they found their places of worſhip thronged by ſuch means, I was, for ſome time, much reſpected by all parties, and did not want encouragement from each party to join them.

BUT the LORD kept me all this while from meddling with the differences and controverſies about the externals of Religion; for I dreaded the conſequences this would produce to ſouls newly awakened. Therefore for many reaſons being perſuaded in my own mind, that I was called to labour as a Member in the national Church, my conſcience did not permit me to diſſent — And when I came to ſee the Bigotry of ſome parties, the lukewarmneſs, and worldly-mindedneſs of others, with their legal method of preaching, &c. I began to bear my teſtimony againſt them, then many waxed cold towards me, others diſputed with me, and thought it as their duty to weaken my hands as much as they could`——— THE

THE enfuing Summer, in the year 1740. as I went through *Glamorganfhire*, I met with Mr. *Seward* at *Cowbridge*, from thence he came on with me to *Cardiff*, then we went on comfortably together, to *Monmouthfhire*, and preached at the feveral Towns of *Newport*, *Caerleon*, *Ufk*, and the Town of *Monmouth*, &c. where Satan was permitted to rage againft us in a moft horrible manner. At *Newport* the Mob rufhed on us with the utmoft rage and fury,——they have torn both my coat-fleeves, and one quite off, and took away my peruke, I being now in the rain ——*O fweet bare headed,*——*under the reproach of* CHRIST! having little filence, I difcourfed on, but foon they hollowed again, and pelted me with apples and dirt, flinging ftones in the utmoft rage about me, I had one blow on my forehead, which caufed a rifing with little blood.——Many friends would have me give over in the tumult, but I could not be free to do that till the ftorm would be over, and GOD be glorified over Satan, &c. When we came to *Caerleon*, every thing feemed calm and quiet, whilft Brother *Seward* prayed and difcourfed fweetly by the Market-houfe; but when I began to difcourfe after him, then they began to roar moft horribly, pelting us with dung and dirt, throwing eggs, plumb-ftones, and other hard fubftance even in our faces, and hollowed fo loud as to drown my voice entirely ——Brother *Seward* had a furious blow on his right eye, which caufed him much anguifh, and as it affected his left, he was obliged to be led by the hand blindfold for some days, — till at last he became totally blind of it. And when we came to *Monmouth*-Town, we had much the same treatment as we had at *Newport* and *Caerleon*, — It happened to be the Horse-race there, both high and low were assembled against us. — And as I began to discourse on a table over against the Town-hall windows, where the Duke of B——, Lord N——, with great number of Gentlemen and Ladies were at dinner, — then they ordered a Drum to be beat by our sides, altho' the LORD enabled me to bear my testimony against their Balls, Assemblies, Horse-races, whoredom and drunkenness, &c. and the Drum continued to beat, and the Mob pelting us with apples, pears, stones and dirt, and a dead dog, &c. During this storm, Brother *Seward* was much afraid of hurt, yet he endured it with much calmness of spirit, saying " Better en-" dure this than Hell." Thus all their opposition could not hinder our progress, — But in the strength of the LORD we went on from conquering to conquer*.

BROTHER *Seward* went with me to *Coleford*, and to *Gloucester*, where we had much power no discourse to many hundreds, both in public and private —

* See *Weekly History*, No 2. printed in *London* in the year 1740. where Mr. *Seward* in a Letter dated from *Trelleck Friday September 12th*, 1740. gives a more full account of the persecution he and Mr. *Harris* suffered at that time in *Monmouthshire*.

Being

Being in *Gloucefter* on a *Sunday*, and hearing that the Sacrament would be at *Nicolas*'s *Church*, I went there; and had a frefh fenfe of my poverty and vilenefs, fo that I could cry experimentally and feelingly, " O Lord, I am the pooreft, the vileft, and the un " worthieft here before thee ——" And when I thus fell at my Saviour's feet, then I had a fweet and clofe communion with him, and my foul felt a pity for all the world, — longing, O! that they all might be born again, and be brought to the true knowledge of the Saviour of finners: yea I felt I deferved hell for not valuing his precious Blood the more! O the infinite value of that Blood! it is the fruit of God's eternal love to poor finners! Here is light, life, and liberty from the guilt and power of fin, &c. and O! that I may abide here forever.

My reception at different places was daily enlarged; although the enemy caufed fome difturbance almoft every where, when at the entreaties of feveral friends, I went to a Revel in *Radnorfhire*, which is an yearly meeting, where numbers of people meet to dance, &c. (I ufually frequented thofe places in order to fpeak to the people, and God was pleafed to blefs the word to the converfion of fome, and conviction of many, who would not attend preaching elfewhere.) After I had began to fhew to the attentive crowd the folly, vanity, and danger of thefe ways, and invited them to the Saviour; I was apprehended by two Juftices; and after I fuffered much contempt and

derifion,

derifion, &c. they drew up their Commitment, &c.
But when they perceived that I was well pleafed to
go to prifon, they fent for fome of my friends to bail
me, which I affented to, leaft they fhould think me
obftinate. So they bound me to appear at the Quarter Seffions, and difmiffed me. When I departed, I
was filled with joy unfpeakable, and great glory —
In confequence of my obligation, I appeared at the
Quarter Seffions, being accompanied by others, who
had anfwered for me; and although we required
our trial, yet they declined it, and obliged us to appear again the next Quarter Seffions.

AT this time, a ftrong attempt was made to take
away my life, as follows; viz. The Hall wherein
the Seffions were held, was an upper room, up a high
flight of ftairs which was oppofite to the Street (and
it being by night) the Mob placed themfelves in a
proper pofture, at the head of the ftairs, to pufh me
down; which defign, if it had taken place, would
have certainly caufed my death, — for they began to
pufh me, but by an efpecial providence, a worthy
Gentleman (one of the Magiftrates on the Bench)
came that moment and fnatched me from their hands;
—and he protected me, and led me to his lodging —
As I was going out of Town, they furrounded me,
and unanimoufly exclaimed againft me, but I was
foon minded to demand peace in the King's name,
upon which GOD ftruck them with fuch an awe,
that I was permitted to efcape ———

THE

THE next Quarter Seffions, when I appeared in Court, an Act was perufed which was made in the Twenty-fecond year of King *Charles* the II. againft feditions and illegal affemblies, that under pretence of Divine worfhip, people met to plot againft the King. when they had done reading it, a Counfellor (being employed by a certain Gentleman) ftood up, at which the whole Court was furprized, he pleaded that thefe affemblies were not fubject to the cenfure and penalties of that Act, unlefs they could juftly charge them with fedition and difloyalty, which they could not poffibly do. Therefore he was clearly of the oppinion that the Defendant might be acquitted of that charge and fufpicion, by his fubfcribing to the Articles of the Church, and taking the oath of alegiance to his Majefty, I immediately expreffed my readinefs to do this, and they thought fit to dif-mifs me. Previous to this time warrants were iffued out to take me, but now the Magiftrates obferved that I was peaceable, and a conformift, and alfo loyal to the King, by which it appeared I was no delin-quent, and not guilty of that which they charged.

IN *Carmarthenfhire*, not far from the County Town, I was interrupted by a certain Knight, who came there purpofely to take me, I fpoke to him, and when he found I was not guilty of what was laid to my charge, I was permitted to give the people a warm Exhortation, being enabled to be faithful, and bold to fpeak in my MASTER's caufe, as well as to

behave

behave with humility; he went away quietly . and
since that time I had peace and quietnefs in this and
in other Counties from the Magiftrates , and the
doors now began to open to feveral confiderable
Towns in *South-Wales*, which were fhut up before.

In the beginning of the year 1741. I went to
North-Wales; and as I proceeded, the enemy was
provoked at my attempt thus to propagate the Gofpel in his territories, and refolved to make a ftand
againft me, and endeavoured, as much as he fhould
be permitted, to take away my life .--having been im-
portuned to vifit *Bala*, in *Merioneth-fhire*, and to proceed to the North, (tho' I had been there once or
twice before) after prayer and confultation, I entruft-
ed God with my life, relying on his faithfulnefs, and
went on. And accidentally, as I was near *Bala*, I
overtook the Minifter that belonged to that place, on
the road, who cautioned me to defift at my peril; I
meekly replied, I was fully perfuaded that it was my
duty, that I had no other intention, but to publifh
the glad tidings of Salvation, and would not wilfully
offend any perfon, &c. However he gave me very
ill language, and came towards me, with a great
club to ftrike me , I told him, when I was reviled,
I was taught not to revile again, and rode on quietly .
—but when I entered the Town, I found a numerous
affembly waiting for me ; —— and it was faid, that
all the County Mob were met together purpofely to
abufe and hinder me—— But at the requeft of my

G

friends I quitted the ftreet, and went to a houfe to difcourfe.

DURING all this I was happy in my foul, and full of power, and courage, my voice being lifted up like a trumpet, fo that the people could hear in fpite of all the difturbance that was made at the door, and window, which was broke to pieces by the Mob; and thus I difcourfed on for fome time. but when the Mob who had been preparing themfelves for the work by exceffive drinking (it was fuppofed that the Minifter had given them the drink) came among the people, a friend defired me to leave off, tho' I was yet full of power in my fpirit, yet preferring my friend's advice before the call in my own foul, I ceafed to fpeak, but I immediately felt the power withdrawn from me;—then I underftood that I had done wrong—However I retired to an upper room, but the Mob, inftead of withdrawing, appeared to be more enraged,—Some furrounded the houfe, whilft others climbed to the top of it, threatening me with death, as foon as I fhould come out. As night drew on, I thought it my duty to go out among them, committing myfelf to the hands of GOD, but as foon as I went out of the houfe, one feized me by the Handkerchief, by it giving way, I was prevented from falling to the ground,——another hit me on the face, whilft others flung ftones and dirt at me, &c. I then thought it was my lot to die *Stephen*'s death

in

in the midft of them , — I fpoke to them, and prayed for them : —— But wh lft I did this, one defired me to go away, telling me that I tempted the LORD by ftaying there, &c. and no fooner I turned my back on my enemies to go away, but I was fome how left to myfelf, and funk under the waves, — though I was not afraid of death, knowing it was an entrance to eternal reft, having no fear of hell, or doubt of GOD's favour through the Blood of CHRIST my SAVIOUR ; yet being rather unwilling to die by the hands of thefe villains, gave me fome uneafinefs, —— they ftill, inhumanly continued to beat me with fticks and ftaffs, and to pelt me with ftones, &c. until I fell under their mercilefs feet, where they continued to beat me until the LORD touched the heart of one of them with pity, or fear of being profecuted for killing me * ; he fwore they fhould beat me no more,

G 2 and

* *The following is a true Account given by men of veracity, of the Judgment of GOD upon fome of the moft cruel perfecutors at that time.*

The perfon that threw the firft ftone to the houfe, in a fhort time afterward, as he was coming home from a fair, fell from his horfe, and broke his back, and foon died Alfo the perfon that was moft cruel for throwing Mr *Harris* headlong down a rock, to a pool about fix yards deep, foon afterward fell within a few yards down that rock, and died on the fpot. Another lufty young man who was a very cruel per-

fecutor

and rescued me out of their hands, whilst they were employed in giving my friends the like treatment; although they were able to make defensive resistance, yet they imitated CHRIST the LORD their Master, in bearing all patiently, as I desired them to do. So at last we came together to our lodging, and dressed our wounds, and there also I exhorted my fellow sufferers, and rejoiced together that we were counted worthy to suffer for CHRIST's sake ——

AFTERWARD I went on my journey to *Caernarvon-shire,* and reached there on a *Saturday*-night; —— *Sunday* morning I enquired where the best church-

secutor on that day, as he was going towards home, fell from his horse upon a stone, fractured his scull, and instantly died. Another person that day, fell down dead in a fit of rage, as he was beating and persecuting in a most inhuman manner; but recovered again that time, and in few years after died miserably, with great remorse of conscience, especially for what he had done on that day. Also another persecutor on his death-bed was so raving-mad that three stout men were not able to hold him from biting his own hands and lips, to pieces, —— and so he died in a most miserable manner. Another when a dying, four persons being with her, who were so terrified at what they had felt and seen in the room with her, that they could hardly abide there, some ghastly apparition was seen on the bed with her, and her pain was so much that she was rising from the bed for fear, &c.

preaching

preaching was, It was faid, it was two or three miles diftance, where the Chancellor preached. I went there, and I heard fuch a fermon as I thought could never come into the heart of man to conceive, or any mouth to utter   he had heard of my coming to *North-Wales*, and took occafion to forewarn the people, leaft I fhould happen to vifit that place. Fiift, he pretended to point me out as a Minifter of the devil, an enemy to GOD, and to the church, and to all mankind, &c. He in feveral refpects defcribed me worfe than the devil, —— becaufe he could not act here but by fuch inftruments, &c. fo he went on, and made a repetition of my being the devil's M nifter, a deluder, a falfe-prophet, &c. and after he had painted me as more worfe than any Monfter Heretic, or the devil himfelf, he fhewed it was a duty incumbent upon the people, out of love to GOD and his church, and their country, to join unanimoufly againft fuch a man, who carried with him fuch deftructive poifon, which would not only deftroy their perfons and eftates, but their immortal fouls forever, &c. But neither he nor the people expected me there fo foon; ——until I went to the Minifter after he came out of church, to fpeak with him about letting up Welfh Schools, &c. and alfo to tell him my difl ke of his fermon; —— then on a mere fuppofition of my being the very perfon publicly expofed in church, the people fet themfelves in order on the way by which I was to go, to take my horfe, that they might

pelt

pelt me with ftones, &c. but though many ftones were flung violently at me, yet the LORD faved me from having any confiderable harm, and kept them from laying violent hands upon me —— Thus I was greatly endangered all this week, and often thought I fhould not be permitted to return alive from this country ——

I returned by way of *Penmorfa* near *Traeth-mawr*; and whilft I waited my paffage, the Mob beftired themfelves againft me, and the fpirit of Murderers were feen in their looks and behaviour, —— they abufed me, —— but being in chains, they could not hurt me much, —— and at laft I efcaped their fury, and came over *Barmouth*-ferry, to a Diffenting Minifter's houfe, in *Merioneth-fhire.* From thence I came by *Machynlleth,* and *Llanbrynmair,* in *Montgomry-fhire,* where my life was endangered again, but was preferved as a prey out of a Lion's mouth —— So I went on and vifited the fouls in that County, who had now began to form themfelves into fmall Societies ——

O what experience I gained by this perilous journey! I never had fo much acquaintance with the nature of felf-love, which grew infenfibly in me, by means of my fuccefs —— I faw more and more of the depth of all evil in my nature, that I often wondered that the earth was permitted to bear fuch a

monfter;

monfter; I daily obferved, and had a clearer evidence of the truth of that expreffion delivered by good Bifhop *Hoper* at the ftake, " LORD, I am " hell, but thou art heaven." I find as yet I am but a child, and fo underftand and fpeak as a child :—— But the LORD by degrees continued to fhew me more of the highth, depth, length and breadth of his love in CHRIST, and led me to know, by experience, more of his fufferings, death, and refurrection, love and faithfulnefs. My eyes were more opened, and my fpiritual underftanding increafed, to apprehend the myftery of JESUS CHRIST, who alone in the various characters we have of him, can be favingly known by the operation of the HOLY GHOST, as the Door, and the Way to GOD, and the ineffable MAJESTY himfelf—— By this light and experience I had deliverance from the Old Covenant and its legal fear, and it drew me alfo more and more under the Law of faith and love, the fruits of the New Covenant, and into Gofpel Liberty; and not licentioufnefs —— The Crofs was burthenfome to my flefh, but I felt my foul growing fweetly under it——

THE following Summer, I was called again to *London*, to affift for fome time at the *Tabernacle*; I made *Briftol* in my way, and going through *Wilt-fhire*, I met with Mr. *Cennick*, and went with him to *Swindon*, and as we preached there, we were fet upon by

the

the Mob to fome purpofe, who went the length of their chain in venting their rage upon us . — They brought horns, guns, and a Fire-engine, &c. —— and when they prefented a Gun to my forehead, my foul was happy, I could chearfully ftand as a mark for them ! One ftruck me on my lip till fome blood came, but GOD was pleafed to endow us with un-common patience and meeknefs, and great power to fpeak to the people, and many liftened with great ferioufnefs —— Then we walked up into the Town, re foning with thofe who oppofed us, — being fmear-ed with mire, gunpowder and the muddy water thrown by the Engine; &c. we were followed by a large concourfe of poor hufbandmen and Traders, &c. and when we had borrowed clothes to change us, and wafhed ourfelves; the people came together in the yard of the houfe where we were entertained; then I preached to them, and Mr. *Cennick* prayed. I am perfuaded fome of them were convinced of fin, and they begged us earneftly to come to a Village about a mile diftant, which we promifed, if GOD would fo permit; and then we went to that Village, where the word of GOD runs and is glorified —— Then I proceeded on my journey to *London.*

IT was very remarkable that we received any material hurt at *Swindon*; — Tho' feveral, in our hearing, bound themfelves by oaths, that we fhould never go away alive, — and they followed us above

a quarter

a quarter of a mile from the Town, but they were not permitted to lay hold of us [1]—

AFTER being fome months in *London*, I returned again, and came through feveral Towns in *England* to *Briftol*, and from thence to *Wales*, in the year 1742. I now faw clearly, that many abufed the liberty of the Gofpel, by turning the grace of GOD into wantonnefs, fuch as fpiritual pride, judging and defpifing others, &c. and becaufe they do not believe that there is perfection, or a deliverance from the effence of fin attainable here, therefore they fit eafy under the power of pride, anger, lightnefs of fpirit, and love of the world, &c. When I faw this, I had a new light and power to preach the genuine fruits of real faith,—and the neceffary confequences of every divine truth favingly believed in the heart;—and to diftinguifh between nominal and real Chrift-ians, &c. and the abfolute neceffity of exhorting and perfuading all to make their calling and election fure,—and to have the victory over all their fpiritual ene-mies, &c. This doctrine caufed a vehement oppofi-tion; but I was encouraged by feeing daily the good effect it had on the fincere, to roufe, purify, and de-live them to the LAMB of GOD ———

I ftill remained a member of the church of *Eng-land*, tho' I am blamed for my Conformity by people of all denominations,—yet I cannot but rejoice on

H

this

this account, and of the good work that the LORD began in the eſtabliſhed Church; and I hope it is a leaven that will effectually operate. I recommend the peaceable ſpirit that remains ſtill in the eſtabliſhed Church, which tolerate ſuch as differ from it,—and does not quench this ſmall efforts of a revival in it; I look on this as a token for good to me——— I find his preſence always in the worſhip and ordinances, and have great freedom to wreſtle in prayer for it, and a ſtrong confidence that GOD would receive, and revive this work in it, &c. However, in this faith and perſuaſion only I can teſtify that I was called to abide in it, ———and not on account of any prejudice, againſt any other party, I abode in it to this day. Several were going to the *Diſſenters*, and other parties,——— and I thought it my duty to declare againſt them,———by laying the following reaſons, and ſcripture-proofs before them: as the example of the prophets of old, and good men, who abode in the *Jewiſh* church, notwith-ſtanding its degeneracy in every reſpect,—and our SAVIOUR and his Apoſtles attended Service at the hour of prayer, in the ſame church,—though they knew, that that church was to be aboliſhed,—nor did the Apoſtle exhort the ſincere to forſake the *Corinthian* church, notwithſtanding the many irregular-ities therein. And our SAVIOUR, after his aſcenſion, did not adviſe his people in the Seven churches of *Aſia*, to leave that church of which they were mem-bers, and to go to another, no; but to reform that

which

which was blameable, and to become the falt of others, &c. —— So in regard to ourfelves, tho' we are but poor inconfiderable, and defpicable members of this church, yet the LORD hath done great things in the Nation, by this revival, —— and he can make us the falt of this church and nation ——

IN the year 1743, the glory of the Divinity of JESUS CHRIST was more deeply imprelled in my foul than ever; The more I meditate on that Text, *Great is the myftery of godlinefs. God was manifeft in the flefh*, &c. *1 Tim.* III. 16. The more the glory thereof fhineth on my foul — I had alfo much help to fee more of the glory and wonders of the Divinity of CHRIST, by reading a Tract, called, *A Sling and a Stone*, &c. I now was brought to fee more and more wonders in his infinite Incarnation, Life, Blood, Death, and Refurrection ! — with the glory of all his offices ! — and alfo the glory of his church, as being related to fuch a *glorious Perfon* ! fhe is called his Spoufe, Temple, Family, Army, and his Fullnefs, &c But yet, I was not infenfible of the workings of felf, that fet itfelf up againft all his offices, but I had a more vifible view of it in my foul, — by thefe difcoveries (which I had gradually of him, and of myfelf) I was led to find that every truth, when revealed by the Spirit, is practical, and will have its proper influence on the foul, by humbling the finner, and exalting the SA-VIOUR — And as the glory of GOD difplayed in our

nature

nature its Divine rays thus on my foul, I felt, it increafed my faith, and my love became more habitual, my joy more folid, my refignation more intire, my fpirit more fmooth and quiet, and more bowels of compaffion and mercy towards poor finners, &c. — I now alfo learn to underftand feveral fcriptures which I could not fpiritually apprehend before, — and what I faw and underftand in other fcriptures before, I came now to fee a much greater depth and more glory in them, every moment of time alfo became very precious in my fight, —— and all the mifpent time, talents, mercies and gifts, that were not employed by the LORD, and for the LORD, were not only loft, but alfo employed againft him.

IN the year 1744, I was called again to *England*, where I found the glory of our SAVIOUR, breaking forth among the people, and many rifing out of the Law to fee the glory of GOD in the face of JESUS CHRIST, the completenefs of his Atonement, with the myftery and glory of his precious Blood! &c. feeing thefe bleffed truths prevailed, the enemy ftired much within doors, when he could do nothing without by perfecutions, — for feveral acquiefced with the light in their heads, without having it in the heart, &c. wherefore they began to fpeak very unguarded things, — which caufed great divifion, &c. although I believe that many had true faith to feed on the SAVIOUR, — and will live for ever ——

AFTER

AFTER been fome time at *London*, I returned to *Wales*, the thoughts of going to the marriage ſtate was weighty with me at this time, a cloſe examination was laid on my ſpirit, what motives leads me to the Matrimonial ſtate — was it the luſt of the fleſh, the luſt of the eye, or the deceit of riches, &c. and through grace I had myſelf free from theſe things. Then the following words of the LORD by *Jeremia*, Chap. xlv. ver. 5. came with power to my heart, *Seekeſt thou great things for thyſelf? ſeek them not* A light came to me with theſe words, If I was going to the marriage-ſtate for myſelf, and not for GOD and his church, that I was an Idolater —— Then I could not reſt till I felt a reſignation of myſelf in this matter wholly from my own hand to the LORD's, and that he ſhould have his own way and time. Now I ſaw that the marriage-ſtate is a great myſtery to ſuch as are brought together by the LORD, and in that relation, ſuch ſhall know the mutual love that is between CHRIST and his church, and alſo what a great thing it is to be a huſband, father, and a head of family, and how to behave in each place as a man of GOD, and an inhabitant of the *new Jeruſalem*.

AT laſt after much prayer, ſelf-examination, and alſo great oppoſition, I was joined in matrimony with *Anne* the Daughter of *John Wiliams* of SARELN, Eſq; *June* 18th, 1744. She was called by my Miniſtry ſome years before, the LORD then gave her

faith

faith through that word, *Heb.* xi. 25. *Choosing rather to suffer affliction with the people of God, than to enjoy the pleasures of sin for a season* She was enabled to stand to her choice, and shewed her faith in all her trials —— This is a time ever to be remembered of me, Nine years to this day I received the spirit of adoption to seal my everlasting salvation.

AND as my spirit increased more and more in beholding the glory of that GOD-MAN, (whom I now beheld clearly the wonder of all worlds, —— the terror of devils, —— the delight of angels, and the real and only hope of poor sinners) then I began to find great and strong opposition to my preaching his Godhead and death, &c. especially in *Wales,* this opposition gained ground, and began to be oppenly opposed, —— and also by many that once called themselves my spiritual children. ——

AND about the year 1746, I saw another spirit of sifting creeping into the work, which was yet different from that which had been before ; viz. the spirit of levity, pride, foolish-jesting, unwatchfulnefs, and carnal rejoicing, —— and that took place immediately after extensive frames and transports, the effects of nature, —— which many seemed to enjoy at the hearing of the word, and singing, &c. and the real and serious spirit that began the work, was at length almost extinguished. —— This lay with weight upon my heart, together with the additional weight of my own in-
firm-

firmities ; — feeing the enemy advancing as a flood, and gaining ground ; — and now very likely to do that in which he had failed once by all the outward oppofition —— The fpirit of awakening finners in the Miniftry was alfo loft, in great meafure, together with its real and folid fruits in the fpirit and the hearts of men ; —— in a word, the fpirit that began and carried on the work for a while, was feemingly vanifhing gradually away —— Many faw this, and were concerned, — and are waiting for his returning to renew the work —— Yet we proceeded in *Wales*, notwithftanding the great jarrs and difputes that arofe amongft us ——

But the year following, the enmity grew ftronger againft the preaching of God's humiliation and death, &c. ftill I bore all in hopes of feeing this ftorm ceafing, as I had feen many others — I now alfo beheld very evidently a tendency in the miniftry to pleafe men, — and to appear wife and popular in the world, — &c. And a great many of my neareft friends both in *Englana* and *Wales*, loofing their former fimplicity, altho' the numbers of Teachers were increafing daily.   I have found alfo that the fpirits of many grew whole, great, and proud, &c. and would not take the word of reproof or exhortation —— altho' they called me their Father, and really was fo, as I began the work in this laft revival, efpecially in *Wales*; —— tho' I have fpent a great part of my time in
England,

England, to spread abroad the fame of the dear Saviour —— I travelled through the several Counties
of *Kent, Essex, Buckingham, Wilt, Sommerset, Gloucester, Oxford, Warwick, Salop,* and *Herefordshire,*
and all the Counties of *Wales*; being much im-
portuned to go to *Scotland* and *Ireland.*

I should not have mentioned these things so particularly, had I not feared that I might rob God of
the glory due to him, for helping me thus far, and
here I must set up my *Ebenezer.* I am at writing
this in the year 1749. being thirty-five years of age,
three seven of which I spent in vanity, and in the
two last seven years, I was called by our Lord, and
followed the Lamb of God.

My good Lord, as I have already said, gave me
(without pre-meditation) the necessary light, utterance and bodily strength instantaneously, whenever
I was to discourse. He enabled me seven years to
do this, mostly out of doors in all weathers, every
day (very few excepted) generally three or four times,
and frequently five times, to ride from eight to
twenty *Welsh* miles (twenty of which are equal to
thirty *English* miles) and upwards) over hills and
dangerous places, through floods, ice and snow, and
He preserved me, that I never received any material
hurt, tho' I often fell from my horse, &c.

I do not write this as a rule for others to copy after, but as a relation of simple truth concerning
what

what the LORD had done in carrying me on hitherto; and therefore I leave it to him to ufe what I write as he fhall pleafe.

AT this time I was continually grieved by the thick darknefs and fpiritual ignorance of many profeffors in the myftery of our SAVIOUR, and by the felfifhnefs and carnality of others, who were favoured with great views of his humanity and glory, and the impatience of thefe different fpirits with each other; feeing all this, my fpirit often longed to finifh my work, and to quit the troublefome ftage of this life, to be with my dear SAVIOUR in the land of peace——

TOWARDS the end of the year 1749, I went to *London*, and in *January* 1750, I parted with my friends and Brethren there, imploring them to attend to the LORD only, and to preach his Godhead and death with power, to the hearts of the hearers, as the only true foundation to build upon ——In my coming down to *Wales*, I faw and felt more than ever of the infinity of our SAVIOUR, in his birth, life, and fufferings, the infinity of his Law and Gofpel; and the infinity of his pardoning grace and fmiles—— wanting nothing indeed but him. I loved him in all his works, but more efpecially in all the fteps of his wonderful humiliation! I had fuch a view and fenfe that I fhould foon be, to all eternity, with him, that tho' I longed for the happy time, yet I faw a thoufand years as nothing to wait for fuch a blifs——

AT

AT this time, I felt more of the difficulty of the work I was engaged in, viz. of dealing with souls aright, and of bringing them to the knowledge of the true GOD in CHRIST, and to direct them only to that great SHEPHERD of souls ——— I obtained also a knowledge of the necessity of seeing and knowing the state of all I discoursed with, and of whom I had the care, and to learn to make a difference, by giving to each what was proper and suitable for their good, according to the state they were in, — As babes, little children, young men, Fathers, or perhaps carnal men, in the house of GOD, who were not as yet begotten to a lively hope that babes should be properly nourished, as redeemed with most precious Blood, and who are exceedingly dear on that and many other considerations to the SAVIOUR that little children also should be properly instructed, disciplined, nursed, that they might grow up according to the Father's purpose. and that young men in CHRIST should have all regard shewn unto them, as being due to their situation (and not too much) respecting places, work, and military weapons which they assume: and the fathers in *Israel* that are called to be rulers and pillars in his house, to have their just place, authority, and esteem , ——— this helped much to make my place and incumberance very weighty to me, and made my spirit to cry, *Who is sufficient for these things ?*

THUS

THUS alſo was ſhewn more clearly to me in many inſtances the greatneſs and difficulty of the work, eſpecially the ſpiritual work of the Miniſtry, and the life of faith , and how (by ſomething in nature, appearing like faith, love, and humility) ſouls are deceived, and think themſelves changed and born again, and that they adorn the Goſpel, &c.——when it is really nothing elſe but what our SAVIOUR termed, the whited walls, and painted ſepulchers. Nature, being only outwardly changed, enlightened, and influenced, yet not without ſome influence of the ſpirit of GOD, ſo that there was ſome ſenſations of joy and ſorrow which ſuch perſons were not accuſtomed to, and they take this to be a Goſpel faith, and real change, but it proves at laſt nothing but a change in the fleſh, and a houſe built on the ſand ——whilſt ſelf-love and the ſpirit of the world lies deep under all, and the ſtrong man armed was never caſt out, for he ſtill, tho' hiddenly, kept GOD's ſeat in the heart,——and thus tho' the ſpirit of ſuch was never awakened by GOD's voice, neither thro' the Law nor Goſpel yet he thinks, perhaps, that he has experienced the real power of both, yet the heart was never convinced ſpiritually of unbelief (altho' the underſtanding has been enlightened to receive ſome new notions) nor has he been convinced of the evil of ſpiritual and ſecret ſins, of his own total fall by nature, and his ignorance of the SAVIOUR and his Blood,——ſuch

I 2

ſuperficial

superficial profeffors fhould tremble leaft when trials come, notwthftanding all their profeffion, and fuppofed faith in the SAVIOUR, they may be ready to join in that blafphemous cry of the *Jews*, " *This man* " *fhall not reign over us———,*" or, " *How can this* " *Man give us his flefh to eat ?*"

I was brought more and more to fee the deceitfulnefs that is in man, how nature may appear like grace, being improved and checked, and feemingly rectified by having the courfe of it turned from delighting itfelf in the common way of the world, of pleafures and honour, &c to run in a religious channel; now delighting itfelf in hearing Sermons, and finging Hymns, efpecially in having the paffions enflamed, never confidering, whether they were truly rooted and grounded in CHRIST, but only feemed to be ftrengthening, eftablifhing, and building each other up in the faith, and imagined that they were thus growing in grace, &c. whileft evidently the fpirit of their minds ftaid behind in the world, had neither power nor authority over the fpirit of the world, nor retained that diftance from it which once they perhaps fought, and yet they fhewed the fame appearance of faith, love, and zeal as formerly —

Now feeing things in this light, a neceffity was laid upon me to lift up my voice like a trumpet to all profeffors to examine their profeffion, and to make a clofe fearch in what the foundation of their religion and

and faith was feated. whether in the outward man, called the flesh or nature, or whether it had indeed penetrated to the inward man, called the heart or spirit?—I faw clearly that there is fuch a thing as krowing CHRIST after the flesh, by a kind of prophetical knowledge and views of him at a diftance, fuch as *Balaam* had, and from thofe views, have a certain confidence in him, and a kind of love to him, and feemingly great joy and happinefs (as the feed on the ftony ground) and yet the heart be whole, felf-righteous, and worldly amidft all this; and the fpirit carnal, afleep, and unawakened, in bondage *to the god of this world* , being never convinced of the fin of nature, and the evil of unbelief, and the difficulty of believing in the SAVIOUR as a finner, and of obeying the call given to fuch in the gofpel, they look back to fomething that they done or felt at different times, and from hence they draw the conclufion, that they are in the covenant, and belong to GOD, and fhall therefore be faved——.

I faw plainly that this was the religion of moft profeffors, they formed a faith to themfelves without coming as loft damned finners to the crofs, and looking to him as the *Ifraelites* looked to the Brazen-Serpent, fleeing to CHRIST, as the man fled from the avenger of blood into the City of Refuge. No wonder then, when this confidence is fettled,

that

that the fpiritual life, the daily combat, the victory of faith, the feeding on the flefh and blood of GOD our SAVIOUR, the myfteries of his Perfon, as GOD and Man, opened in all his obedience and humiliation, and the infinite depth of his glorious riches, and the wonders of his Blood and wounds ! with the infinite torments which he endured , no wonder, I fay, that thefe myfteries remain a fecret to them, and affords no life or entertainment to them ; — but become matters of fpeculation and controverfy, if not ridicule,—inftead of being their life, delight, and daily food —

THE more my fpirit was raifed to the LORD, to fee the value of his precious Blood, the more neceffity I faw of having that Fountain daily to wafh me, and all I did ; and alfo to teftify to all of this Fountain, which alone cleanfes from all fin, and by which alone we overcome — By feeing and feeling this in my own foul, I had caufe to fear and to fufpect the religion of many, whom I hoped formerly were come to *Mount Sion*, and to the Blood of fprinkling, that the Strong-man armed had not been caft out, but had only gone out for a time — and that the natural enmity of the firft *Adam*, and the fpirit of the old Covenant (which is oppofite to the new Way, of falvation by the Blood and death of a SAVIOUR) had not been caft out and mortified , — But after all that GOD had done on and for them, they were no more

than

than outward-court worſhippers ; — tho' many cried, we are *Abraham's* children, viz. GOD's people,
a choſen generation, called of the LORD , — but
ſuch nomination of ourſelves is not ſufficient, when
the LORD denies us, as not being born of him.

THEN I was led often to ſhew, what was the
works and actions of *Abraham's* faith , — being dead
to his poſſeſſions and country, &c he realy obeyed
the call, and went out to wander in a ſtrange land,
among Heathens, not knowing whither he went , —
And alſo denied himſelf, forſook his own reaſon, —
by believing what appeared impoſſible, viz that he
ſhould have a ſon from a barren womb, now ripe for
earth, — And again by offering up that ſame *Iſaac*
(who was the delight of his heart and deſire of his
eyes, &c.) on a mere command without having any
ſatisfaction given to the carnal enquiries of his reaſon ; — which noble works and actions our SAVIOUR
ſhewed to the *Jews* when he was on earth, and is
now left upon record for all his ſpiritual ſeed likewiſe.
Alſo I often ſpoke of the *Iſraelites*, how many thouſands of them died in the wilderneſs, for that damnable ſin of unbelief, not taking GOD on his word,
and not venturing on the promiſe in the face of all
difficulties from giants, walled towns, and fenced
cities——O how unbelieving they were, notwithſtanding all the wonderful works which he had done
for them in *Egypt*, at the Red-ſea, and in feeding
them with Angel's-food ſo many years in the wilderneſs,

nefs, and fhewing his love and favour to them above all the nations on the earth; and tho' he had fo often pardoned them by the entreaties of *Mofes*, efpecially by his putting him in mind of his bleffed Name and glory, and how the nations would blafpheme, and fay, that he could not after all bring them to *Canaan* where he intended —— But their ftubborn unbelief made him at laft to fwear in his wrath that they fhould never enter into his reft ——

THESE and the like confiderations made me fhed many tears over profeffors, leaft it fhould be their cafe,——*for all thefe things happened unto them for enfamples, and they are written for our admonition* I Cor. x. 11. As *Paul* applies it to the Chriftian Church; tho' this cannot take place litterally under the Gofpel difpenfation, yet fpiritually, it might be the cafe of every individual profeffor, or of a party of profeffing Chriftians, therefore it ferves as a warning to all, left fpiritually the fame judgment fhould ftill overtake us, after all his kind dealing towards us, —— we fhould tremble left our fpirits ftay behind in the world, and come not to the SAVIOUR continually, but go on building on his paft favours, inftead of obeying his prefent call to go on (venturing on him and his word) from conquering to conquer, to take poffeffion on the Land of Promife, the dear SAVIOUR and his glorious Kingdom, in fpite of all oppofition that rife and fet themfelves againft us, both from our corrupt nature and others, &c.

SEEING

SEEING this self and carnal spirit getting ground, and growing under the seemingly glorious work that was going on, and professors willing to content themselves with false peace—overlooking their sins,—being not truly brought (by the Holy Spirit daily) under a deep sense of them to the cross of CHRIST, to see them there punished, forgiven, and done away in his Blood. Superficial light and knowledge can never penetrate to this spiritual discovery of our sins thus laid upon GOD our SAVIOUR. Neither can it feed, and derive all its life and comfort from his sufferings and death. And seeing so many resting, short of this discovery, in what they received from the LORD, and not relying by faith on CHRIST, and what he had done and suffered for us ; I had reason to fear, there were but few born again — for where a new man is formed, it must have the Bread of Life, CHRIST himself, he cannot be satisfied with hearing of him, he must have HIM, for his constant object , to speak with, and to delight in him , and must have his Body and Blood daily for his meat and drink , in a word, his REDEEMER must be his all, upon whom he rests. And those who are rightly and truly awakened, to believe what the LORD says of the miserable state of man by nature, without being made a new man, in CHRIST JESUS ; cannot rest any where, without coming to JESUS, and knowing him for themselves , and that he is their SAVIOUR, and what he had done and suffered for them, is become their continual meat and drink, on which they feed , and thus they come up out of the wilderness, leaning on their Beloved.

K   SEEING

PERCEIVING thus that the work was not effectually carried on, I could not but found the alarm, and cry aloud, *O Watch-men! O Watch-men! What of the night! What of the night!* I had authority through the Spirit of GOD, to declare againſt the Tares, growing in the LORD's garden. And at the ſame time calling ſinners to the great Attonement in the Blood of CHRIST. And ſhewing alſo how the ſin of ſecretly deſpiſing it, or thinking of it carnally as common blood, is the greateſt of all ſins, ———and that GOD will not deal with us ſinners, but in, and through CHRIST's Blood; —and as the *Jews* dared not to come before him, without the blood of the ſacrifice, offered in the Temple, how can we then, preſume to deal with GOD, without the Blood of CHRIST? and as it is not only ſome times that ſatan and our evil nature do ſet upon us to tempt and defile us, but they do it continually (if we rightly feel and know what paſſes) then are we continually under an abſolute neceſſity of having CHRIST's Blood to waſh and cleanſe us from our ſins, and his Spirit to renew our ſouls. O the infinite and wonderful efficacy of CHRIST's moſt precious Blood! How it fills the whole creation! and has infinity in it, becauſe it is the Blood of GOD! by which he Redeemed his Church, and cleanſes his people, from all their ſins.

As the LORD himſelf ſent me round the Country at my firſt ſetting out, and gave me a deſire to pleaſe him only, and helped me to ſpeak plain truths,

ſo

fo at this time, a neceffity was laid upon me to preach that great truth which he revealed to my own foul, viz. the wonderful condefce fion and myftery of GOD, in our nature, reconciling the world to himfelf, not imputing their fins, — That he was GOD in the womb of *Mary*, when HE affumed our nature, laying in himfelf the foundation of our falvation and deliverance — and was the Supreme GOD in his poor birth and fwaddling clothes! and in all his fufferings, that He was the great I AM! the ALPHA and OMEGA! and that there is none other GOD but him! There are Three Perfons, but one GOD, and thofe that worfhip another GOD, befides him, do worfhip an Idol, — for *in him dwelleth all the fulnefs of the Godhead bodily!* and when the time came to make an Attonement for our fins, when He, the great Sacrifice, was raifed on the Altar of the crofs, all nature, earth, and hell, was in an uproar or confufion, — the Sun was darkened, the earth trembled, the dead awoke, and were raifed, &c. that all might enquire, What is the caufe and meaning of all this?

"'TIS THE MIGHTY MAKER DIES!"
Dr. *Watts.*

I went on thus fome years through *Wales*, bearing my teftimony to thefe truths, in the face of carnal profeffors, *Arians* and *Socinians*, who all railed againft me, — Altho' it proved to be an occafion of much murmuring, contention, and divifion, yet I am in a lively hope, that the LORD will blefs his own truths, in his proper time, it may be when I am gone —

K 2   I was

I was then in great expectation, that it would be my laft work and teftimony——But, at his feet I leave myfelf, together with my performances, and labour, and to him I commit myfelf, alfo, for the remainder of my life, knowing that he is able for the time to come, to carry me through every trial, work or fuffering, as he has done hitherto, and thro' his unchangeable grace, to the chief of finners, I fet up my *Ebenezer* And though I know but little of CHRIST the LORD as I fhould, yet I am a living witnefs of his free grace, and of what is faid of him in the fcripture, therefore I could refrain but inviting all to fubmit to his righteoufnefs, and government of grace, and to wait at his gate, that they might be made happy forever in Him, the only fure Reft and fhelter for poor penitent finners. He is the only City of refuge, the only friend, for diftreffed fouls to flee to, and the only one that will never leave them, and will fuit all their need, and can fupply all their wants; and will at laft prefent them fpotlefs to the FA-THER ——

Now I cannot, but afcribe all the glory to him who has loved, pitied, and forgiven me, the chief of finners, indeed in my own eyes, who ftill wafhes and heals me by his precious Blood, and doth over-rule and manage even my very evils to turn them for my good—To him therefore who is worthy with the FATHER and HOLY GHOST, be as is moft due, all honour and glory, by all his Church in time and eternity, Amen, and Amen.

THE

SECOND PART,

COLLECTED by his SUCCESSORS; who were *Eye-witnesses* of his *Proceedings* to his departing into Glory the *Matter* of which is chiefly taken from his *Diary*.

AFTER feventeen years, of hard labour, in the LORD's work through *Wales*, and great part of *England*, Mr. *Harris* fettled at *Trevecka*, where he fpent the greateft part of his time in his own houfe; tho' he made feveral journies from thence in the following years. A few of thofe who received a bleffing through his miniftery, in former years, began to gather to him there; and as he preached to them, two or three times a day, they earneftly defired to ftay there with him. The ardent defire of thefe fincere people, he could not withftand, and thus in *April* 1752, he laid the foundation of the prefent building at *Trevecka*; tho' he had at that time neither friends nor money — he fet about it purely in faith, relying on the LORD, and his promife; having an impreffion in his mind, for fome years paft, that he

fhould

should build a house for GOD—and he set about it in a full persuasion, that the same GOD, who had sent him at first, in an uncommon manner, to awaken the country; also now laid this undertaking upon him. He himself writes thus concerning it.

" I was impelled to build, by the same spirit which " sent me about to preach, and at a time I was far " from being provided with money or friends, for " the latter had deserted me, and instead of the for- " mer, I had demands upon me—and about 40 " workmen to pay, and maintain,—and yet I made " use of no means to get one Shilling, but an hum- " ble pleading of and confiding on the promise; on " which I trust my all, as both for temporal, and " spiritual things."

BUT soon after he began to build, some people came to offer their work and help to him, that they might have a more convenient opportunity to be under his care, and profit by his ministery daily, thus the family began to be gathered together, this year. Mr. *Harris* had at this time a severe fit of sickness, but yet though very weak, he would preach to the people, till he was seemingly, ready to die for fatigue, being not able to move himself from the chair he used to sit in, and speak from, but we were obliged to carry him in it, into his room;—at other times, when he recovered a little, he would call the family to

his

his Bed-room, and would exhort them from his bed, for a long while, the divine bleſſing attending it to their ſouls. He continued ſome months in this fit of ſickneſs, expecting to go home to his dear LORD and SAVIOUR, as he himſelf expreſſes it, " I was all this " time in continual hopes of going home, to my dear " SAVIOUR, and expecting it with Solicitation." And yet all this while he continued to diſcourſe daily to the people, as one already in the ſuberbs of heaven.

IN the year 1753 a part of the building being finiſhed, a great number of people flocked to him from all parts, many of them under conviction, merely to hear the word; and others partly from curioſity, the report of Mr. *Harris's* preaching daily at *Trevecka*, having ſpread throughout all *Wales*, ⸺ Satan alſo began to rage, and ſet the whole country as it were in an uproar ⸺ inventing all manner of lies, &c. that originated in their various ideas of the aim of the multitude crowding to that place. However the people continued to come there from all parts of *Wales*, ſome ſtaying, for a time, others returning home, partly becauſe their preſent circumſtances did not admit of their ſtaying at preſent, partly complaining, ſome that the fare, others that the preaching and diſcipline was too hard, and that Mr. *Harris* was an intollerable reprover, &c. yet for all this, many ſettled there this year, eſpecially ſingle perſons, both men and women; giving themſelves to

the

the LORD and his work, becaufe they believed it was a part of the LORD's work, and fuited to the rules laid down in the Bible.

AT the end of this year, and the beginning of the year 1754, there was a fettled family at *Trevecka*, of about a hundred fettled perfons, befides thofe coming and going, as we hinted before, and Mr. *Harris* took upon him the fole care of their fpiritual and temporal concerns, having nothing outwardly adequate to pro- vide for fuch a family, nor any manufactory fet up, but only a couple of fmall rented farms, and a little quantity of wool bought for the women to fpin, to get their maintenance by — It is a difficult thing to imagine, what ftraits Mr. *Harris* went through at this time, concerning the outward care of the peo- ple only, befides the care of their fouls; preaching publickly, and exhorting privately, daily — watch- ing many nights to pray and wreftle with the LORD, and as foon as the family arofe in the morning, preaching again, exhorting them for hours together, without having had any reft in bed, but yet with frefh power, and fpirit from the LORD —— of this we were living eye-witneffes.

As to outward matters, the LORD has been with him in a furprifing manner, frequently, when a call for payment came to him, he had no profpect in the world, how to difcharge the debt, but applying to the LORD in prayer, and pleading his promife, and

that

that he did not bear thefe burdens for himfelf, but for him, and therefore relying upon him, that he would certainly help and carry him through——And very often the LORD anfwered him in an unexpected manner, by fending fome perfon or other with as much money as he wanted, either as an acknowledgement for the benefit received from this work, or as a loan. Thus the LORD never forfook him ! as he writes, thus,
" Being often in ftraits, concerning temporal things,
" wanting 20*l* or 50*l* or even 100*l*, and hav-
" ing no where to turn to, for affiftance, but to
" the promife; the LORD not relieving till the laft
" pinch, and even then appearing from a quarter
" that none could never imagine, fome bringing, and
" fome fending me 10*l* or 20*l* and even 100*l*
" tho' living at the diftance of 70 or 80 miles,
" being compel'd fo to do, only by the word
" founding in their confcience, night and day, and
" no man in the world knowing, or imagining, any
" thing of it——Thus the LORD appeared for me
" many times——This feems ftrange to many, and
" well it may, yet it is real truth."

IN the year 1755, feveral families came to Trevecka, efpecially from *North Wales*, fome to live in the family, and others to Farms in the neighbourhood, that they might have a more convenient opportunity of attending Mr. *Harris's* preaching. Many of them had fubftance, others were poor, and having many children, were obliged to be affifted. Mr.

L   *Harris*

Harris wrote thus about that time — " No fooner
" was a great part of the building finifhed, but foon
" appeared prefently here and there a family, which
" I neither thought of, nor fent for, nor could
" expect. Therefore it appears evident to me, that
" not man, but the LORD, hath done great things
" for us; many people continued to come here, not-
" withstanding croffes and tryals, to a place, repref-
" ented by all in the blackeft manner, being drawn only
" by love to the truth, and the force of the LORD's
" voice they found to their hearts thro' my miniftry,
" freely leaving their country, and all that was dear to
" them, working, and living hard, and leaving it wholly
" to me to order them, both in their work and fare.
" There are now above 100 perfons, old and young,
" that board, work, and fleep, in the houfe, amongft
" which are ten families; and ten families live out
" in farms, in the neighbourhood."

THE plain truths which they formerly heard by
Mr *Harris*'s miniftery, brought thofe people thither
from all parts of *Wales*, and fome even from *England*
alfo And when they came to refide there, many
of them teftified, that the word of GOD, as preached
by Mr. *Harris*, was attended with more and more
energy and benefit to their fouls, and alfo that they
faw a neceffity of being under the LORD's difcipline,
as well as under the preaching of the word, efpecially
as the LORD hath appointed it in his word, that his
fervants fhould meet in fellowfhip, and ufe other

means

means of grace, for the benefit of his people. And that every true minister of the Gospel should be both a watch-man and overseer, to look after the flock, *Acts* xx. 28. and a preacher of the word unto them, 2 *Tim* iv 2.

At the end of this year, there was about 120 persons in the family, besides those families in the neighbourhood, that belonged to it. Mr. *Harris* preached publickly two or three times daily, to the family; besides keeping private meetings with one part or other of them, an hour every day of the week. They gave themselves thus to the LORD, and to his servants by the will of GOD, as the HOLY GHOST directs us to do. 2 *Cor.* viii. 5. From the beginning of this work, the LORD had moved and fitted out two or three Exhorters, as assistants to Mr. *Harris*, to exhort, both at home and abroad — and by this time, the LORD had raised others as helpers both, in the ministry, and government of the family

In the year 1756, our SAVIOUR began to gather some fruit from his little Garden at *Trevecka*; some souls departed very happily, to eternity, praising, and testifying of JESUS, how dear, and precious he was to them in their dying moments, that they beheld eternity bright and glorious before them, through the Blood of CHRIST, Blessing him, for his love and grace, and for having brought them to *Trevecka*, where they found edification for their souls, &c. This afforded much comfort and joy to them that were yet

left

left here below, in this vale of misery, seeing their dear brethren and sisters depart, strong in faith, to their eternal home.

THIS year, as the Nation was engaged in war with *France*, Mr *Harris* was in much concern, least our priviledges and liberties should be taken away from us; especially the liberty of the Gospel, which should the *Papists* succeed, we should be robbed of. He laid this matter therefore before the family, especially the young men, had any of them a willing mind and spirit to go to the service of our good king, against Popery, entreating them to be earnest with the LORD in prayer, for his aid and defence, at this critical juncture, and soon after he had proposed this matter, many of them unanimously answered, that they were willing and ready; and it was then settled, that five young men should go to the army, they went in faith, and the strength of the LORD, willing to lay down their lives, for the liberty of the Gospel *.

IN

---

* THESE five young men went from *Trevecka*, to *Hereford*, where they joined the 58th regiment, and from thence to *Plymouth*, till orders came for them, to embark for *Ireland*, and as the heat of the war between us and the *French*, was chiefly then in *America*, further orders came for that regiment to embark for *America*, so they embarked at *Cork*, and landed at *Halifax*, in *Nova Scotia* The first engagement they were in, was at the sieging of *Louisbourg*, and taking it, the next indefatigable enterprize they were in (under the command of brave General *Wolfe*, who then lost his life) was the taking of *Quebec*, which with

all

IN the year 1757, many people continued to come to *Trevecka*, tho' many alfo went away, after being there for a while. In this, and the two following years, above forty perfons died in the family, which in fome fenfe, was a great lofs, and feemingly a fore-runner of fome change amongft us , but the bleffing which attended their departure, made this lofs a great gain, not only to them that died, but to the living alfo , feeing the LORD's grace and faithfulnefs to them in their laft hours, enabling them to triumph over death, and all their enemies , thanking him for all the means, he vouchfafed to make ufe of, to bring them to a true feeling fenfe of themfelves, as finners, and a knowledge of CHRIST as their SAVIOUR ———

OF the perfons who died in thofe years, there were fome children, from feven to twelve years old, moftly
of the

all the Country, is now in the poffeffion of the *Englifh*. The laft place they took, was the *Havana*, from the *Spaniards*, which was the laft blow in that notable war.

THE LORD JESUS was with their fpirits in a furprifing man-ner they kept clofe together in watching and prayer, reading the Bible, exhorting one another, and their fellow foldiers. They wrote home from *Quebec*, that they had the fpirit of pray-er and reliance on the LORD, even in the heat of the battles ; becaufe, fay they " We are in his care, and entered upon this " way of life for him, fighting againft Popery, in defence of our " Gofpel priviledges, &c." Thus, they were kept by our SA-VIOUR, contented and happy in their fpirits, and in their bodies alfo, not receiving any material hurt ——

IT

the small-pox, some of the children praised the LORD
JESUS in a surprising manner, testifying, "that They
"loved him, because he suffered and died for them—"
Mr. *Harris* also was powerfully enabled to pray with
many of them, in their dying moments. And we are
living witnesses of this, that the Spirit of the LORD
was present, comforting, and removing the fear of
death from them, which some of them at first sorely
complained of—but they then longed to behold
his face, and be forever with him.

IT is worthy of notice, that four of those young men died a
natural death, in that part of the world, two of them dyed, and
were buried at *Halifax*, very happy in their spirits, believing
and testifying of the LORD JESUS, that he is faithful to his
promise, &c The third dyed at Sea, in the voyage to *Havana*, the fourth at the *Havana*, after taking it——

THE fifth, was taken prisoner by the *French*, and after being
for some weeks a prisoner in *France*, when peace was concluded,
he came to *England*, and had an offer of preferment, but chose
rather to come home, so he came directly to *Trevecka*, where
he was gladly received by all the family—as it was a matter of
great joy and gladness to see him, after being absent seven years,
but more especially, as the LORD's presence was, and has been
with him, keeping him, not only, from the vice and wickedness,
which most commonly prevails in the army, but was also kept
with the LORD in spirit, growing in the grace of our LORD
JESUS CHRIST, and brought a most pleasing account of them
that finished their course, and of the faithfulness of the LORD
JESUS to himself, and to them, in all their trials He is still
alive, and continues an honest faithful servant in the house of
GOD, and has much to speak, as an Exhorter, about the grace
of the good Shepherd of *Israel*—carrying a musket-ball in his
leg, yet still is very happy and contented, a living witness of the
LORD's faithfulness, and goodness

ABOUT

ABOUT the fpring of the year 1759, Mr. *Harris* wrote thus, " We have buried fince the beginning " of this work, above forty perfons, and there are " ftill about the fame number in the family, and " about thirty in the farms. The word has been " preached hear, I truft, with power and authority, " three times a day, and four times every Sunday, " this feven years. Surely, I can fay, that this is the " LORD's work, for he has hitherto been pleafed " to own it, by bringing and keeping people here; " and by giving me a fpirit of faith to ftand in " the face of my own, and other's fins, and many " other impoffibilities, —— He hath honoured us in " ftanding by, and protecting amidft many heavy " ftorms, that indeed would have defeated all natural " ftrength, and overturned all that was not built on " the Rock Here, therefore, I can fet up an *Eben-* " *ezer*, and fay, *Thus far the* LORD *hath helped me.* " This is the LORD's doing, this work was founded, " carried on, and fupported by the LORD, and " that by his free grace, and not by the wifdom and " policy of any man, nor by the arm of flefh — and " though Satan would be glad, to deftroy it, yet it " remains ftanding, and flourifhing, in fpite of all " difficulties from without, and fin, divifions, and " rebellions within."

TOWARDS the end of this year, when the Nation was alarmed with an invafion intended from *France*, Mr. *Harris* fhewed much concern about the welfare

of

of the kingdom in general, and our rites and privileges both public and private. About that time, some of the Gentlemen of the County, offered him a commiſſion in the *Breconſhire* Militia; he then anſwered, that he could not agree with the offer, but upon condition, thit they would give him liberty to preach the Goſpel, where ever he ſhould go — and told them farther, that his chief motive, and concern in that affair, was the danger he ſaw the liberty of the Goſpel, and our priviledges in, of being taken from us; and having been for many years in danger of his life, for preaching the word of GOD, in many places, he was even now willing to lay down his life, if occaſion required, to defend it, but that if he ſhould ſerve as a ſoldier for king *George*, that he muſt have liberty to preach the Goſpel, of KING JESUS — The Officers aſſenting to theſe motives, and inſiſting upon his accepting the office — He replied again, that he muſt pray to the LORD for knowledge of his mind and will, and have the conſent of his large family; to which alſo they made no objection.

THUS, after waiting on the LORD in prayer, he was fully perſuaded in his mind, that the ſame ſpirit of GOD, who ſent him at firſt to preach the word, in an uncommon manner, would ſend him now in the like extraordinary way to defend it, and to offer his life for the truth he preached, and the liberty we enjoy in this kingdom. He laid the matter thus before the family, imploring the aſſiſtance of their

prayers,

prayers, how to act on this critical affair; and also, whether any of them had an inclination to go for the LORD's fake, with him, to offer their lives in defence of the Gofpel, &c. The matter was then further confidered, and laid before the LORD in prayer, by the whole family — And all confented that Mr. *Harris* fhould go, believing it to be the will of GOD —— many alfo of the men were willing to go with him, and to lay down their lives, for the protection of the precious word of GOD, if occafion required ; and the reft of the family willingly refigning him, and the men that intended to accompany him.

Mr. *Harris*, having fettled all at *Trevecka*, and delivered the affairs of the family, into the hands of Truftees, he went intending to ferve the LORD, and his king, even unto death, together with Twenty four men of the family, twelve of them as volunteers, on Mr. *Harris*'s own coft, arms, cloathing, and maintenance, for three years : — They imbodied with the *Briconfhire* Militia, in the beginning of the year 1760. Mr *Harris* received an Enfign's commifion at his enterance into the Battalion, but afterwards was made a Captain. Before we proceed, we muft infert a few lines, that he himfelf wrote them at this time, on the value of the word of GOD, the Bible.

" I am refolutly, and cooly determined to go freely,
" and confcientioufly, and die in the field of Battle in
" defence of the precious word of GOD, the Bible,
" againft Popery, —— Who can fufficiently fet forth

the

" the value of a Book, wherein GOD fpeakes? and
" that to all ranks, degrees, ages, and languages
" of men? who can fet it forth in its own real
" and majeftic Glory? O the Infinite, and unfathom-
" able depth of Glory and Divine wifdom and love
" in it! The glory of the fun is nothing in com-
" parifon to the Glory of this valuable treafure!
" which is indeed the mouth, and Image of GOD
" himfelf, drawn by himfelf! — A Book, which He
" has made the ftandard, touch-ftone, and rule to
" try, even his own work by! whereby all fpirits,
" doctrine, miniftry, and church dicipline, all faith,
" love, truth, and obedience are proved! A Book
" that GOD has referred all men to, from the Mon-
" arch to the peafant, — The Univerfal teacher of all
" men ——— Here is the feed whence the church and
" her faith are begotten, —and herein is fhe purified,
" and nurfed, here is the bel ever's armoury, herein is
" the true ineffable Light of the world, herein the
" unerring Father and teacher of all, fpeaks both to
" young and old, high and low, rich and poor,—here
" man's pride is humbled, his wounds fearched, The
" SAVIOUR revealed, and declared to be made ours!

" IF Life, and its various comforts and neceffar-
" ies are vaftly dear, How much more fhould this
" treafure be? without it there is no faith, nor Sal-
" vation. — By this, we know, what could not be
" known by any other way or means, and that with the
" greateft certainty, both of GOD, and of ourfelves,

" of

" of prefent and future exiſtance , without this, all is
" uncertain, and thick darkneſs , this alone, ſpeaks
" infallibly, and calls for implicit faith.   O that its
" Glory may fill this Nation, ——— Happy the man
" that ſhall be counted worthy to ſhew forth this
" univerſal teacher, in its own uncovered Majeſty, ——
" It would be an unſpeakable ſervice both to GOD
" and man, ——— and wou'd defeat all hell, and cut
" its way thro' all difficulties , and as the Infinity and
" Majeſty of GOD, its Author, will gradually be dif-
" played to our hearts, ſo will this, his vicegerent on
" earth, this, his manner of ſpeaking to us, making
" himſelf, and his mind of Grace, known to us ; and
" by this means, working in us, *both to will and to do*
" *of his good pleaſure,* Phil. ii. **13** and eſtabliſhing his
" kingdom among us, and in us, and bringing Glory to
" himſelf by our ſalvation   be perpetualy come more
" intelligible and precious to us — without this, we
" are without hope, without knowledge of our Miſery
" or Recovery, &c.   O the ineffable Treaſure ! ——
" no wonder ſo many thouſands triumphed in dying
" for the precious Bible — Now I go freely, without
" compulſion, to ſhew the regard I have for the
" priviledges we enjoy, under our beſt of kings, ———
" our Ineffable priviledges, eſpecially the precious
" Goſpel of our SAVIOUR, contained in the whole
" Book of GOD, which now is openly read through-
" out the kingdom   every perſon being ſuffered to
" exhort his neighbour without moleſtation ———

"I commit my Family to he LORD, and am
" going, with a part of it (who freely offered their
" lives on this occasion) to defend our Nation and
" priviledges, and to shew publickly, that we are dead
" to all things hear below, — or at least, that we can
" part with all for the sake of our dear LORD and
" SAVIOUR, even with Life it self, —— and that we
" seek a City above." *Heb* XIII. 14.

THUS He went, and left at *Trevecka* above 120
persons in the family, who all willingly resigned him
and the men to the LORD, some wives willingly resigned their dear Husbands, resolving to cleave to the
LORD, by giving themselves wholly to him, believing
that he would take care of them. And indeed, we have
experienced that he has been with us as a tender
Father; and owning us before the world as his
people, and that the LORD JESUS was our SAVIOUR
and GOD; and not Mr. *Harris*, as people used to
say.

NOTWITHSTANDING many trials from with in
and without, the LORD was with us, and kept us together, — The Preaching and the meetings were
kept daily as before, and the outward affairs, went on
regularly the same. We were visited by two severe fits
of sickness, when Mr. *Harris* was abroad, and in
one of them, no less than fifty persons lay sick at the
same time, and even some of those that were over the
care of the family, — it being the time of Harvest, —

yet

yet the LORD brought us through, even at this critical feafon, that every thing turned out very well; and indeed the fick and the healthy had a happy time, and the prefence of the Son of GOD being amongft us; He that appeared in the fiery-furnace, with the three Brethren, comforted our fick ones, in a particular manner, — and made even this bitter cup, fweet, to the whole family.

BUT to Return, the firft Rout, which Mr. *Harris* and the Militia had, was in the fpring of the year 1760 to *Yarmouth*, a Sea-port Town in *Norfolk*, it having pleafed the LORD, as foon as they arived at *Yarmouth*, to open a door for him to preach there and other places, in his Regimentals, every evening, to many hearers, who feemingly attended to the word, and a bleffing refted upon fome fouls there.

THE following Winter, they returned from hence to *Erecon*, by another Road, which gave him an opportunity to preach in other Towns, &c — And as they made *Brecon*, their Head-quarters, for that Winter, he had an opportunity to be a part of his time now, and then, at *Trevecka*, with his family. The following Summer 1761 they took another Rout to the weft of England, fo that he had a new field for preaching the Gofpel. Then they fettled for a while at *Bidiford* and *Torrington*, where he met with a kind reception, and many hearers.———In the Summer
1762,

1762, He went to several other Populous Towns in the west, as *Barnstable* and *Plymouth*, &c. Where he continued to preach the Gospel at every opportunity.

AFTER being thus three years in the Militia, the war over, and a treaty of Peace concluded, he and his little company, returned to *Trevecka*, after shewing his faith and love to the LORD JESUS, and also his love and loyalty to his king and country. —— He spent the remainder of his life at *Trevecka*, with his large family, — except only some few rounds he took now, and then, to preach, both in *England*, and *Wales*.

IN the year 1764, He agreed with the Vicar, to have a monthly Sacrament, at our Parish church, which had only been administered four times a year, before. On Sunday February 5th 1764, we received the first monthly Sacrament, He wrote thus; " This was a great Day indeed, the first time we " had the communion according to our wish, and " request, and this Priviledge has been given us, in answer to our prayer, and is a further open proof of " our SAVIOUR's Love to us, — We were happy " in the morning, in exhorting, and went happily " together to the Publick service, and I trust in one " spirit, to the LORD's Table," &c.

THE 19th of this month our people sat for the

first

firft time, in the Gallary of the Parifh Church to fing, and ever fince continue to do fo every Sunday. Mr. *Harris* made the following obfervation on this day, " While the people were finging, to day at " Church, fuch a Glory fell on me, and I thought " filled the Church, as words cannot exprefs, —— " We are happy in this, and in many other refpects, " having our publick and private meetings daily, " and on Sundays before going to Church, and when " we return, without any moleftation at *Trevecka*."

AND as the late Revival, in Religion, began in the eftablifhed Church, we think it not neceffary or prudent to feparate ourfelves from it, but our duty to abide in it, and to go to our Parifh Church every Sunday, to join in the prayers, to hear the reading of GOD's word, and to ufe the Ordinances ; we find that our SAVIOUR meets us there, by making them a bleffing to our Souls.

IN the years 1767, and 1768, Mr. *Harris* was very glad of Lady *Huntingdon's* plan, of building a College at Lower *Trevecka*, He began to Repair the old Building there, —— and afterward Rented it to her Ladyfhip, for her College, and when it was finifhed, an inftitution fixed, for training up young men to the Miniftry, Mr *Harris* ufed to go there every day, for a long while, to Exhort, and difcourfe with the young Students, —— trufting it would continue a Spiritual Seminary of Learning, like the School of the Prophets. 2 *Kings* vi. 1, 2.

IN

IN the year 1770, He buried his dear Wife, ſhe
departed very happy in the LORD, and was an
Inſtrument of edification to all about her. After her
death, He decayed more and more in his body, and
in his laſt year, had now and then, very ſevere fits of
the ſtone, which at laſt carried him off. — Yet for
the laſt weeks of his life, He would ſtill come down
to Preach, and Exhort the family, and that alſo
with much Power; — inſiſting much on having a
true and thorough change in the inward man, — and
ſpeaking much againſt ſuperficial Religion, and receiving the truths of GOD in the fleſh, — without
feeling any true Effect on the heart, ſo as to change
the ſpirit and the whole man, to become one ſpirit
with CHRIST, experiencing the power of his re-
ſurrection, and the benefits of his death.

*NOW we ſhall only inſert ſome detached
Reflections, as He wrote himſelf in his laſt
ſickneſs.*

" I find the SAVIOUR's will is my heaven, be it
   " what it may, but have, I think from him,
" inſatiable cries to go home, out of this body, to my
" dear Father, SAVIOUR, and Comforter, O how I
" loved every word that came from the dear SAVIOUR,
" and all his dear people, that feed on him, and re-
" ceive every good thing of him. I feel my ſpirit eats
" his words, and I could waſh the feet of his ſervants,
                                                      " My

" My spirit adored him, for giving me leave to hope,
" for that blessed time, to come into his presence;
" much more for giving me room to hope, that my
" work is done: and that I am at the door, and
" that I, a poor sinner, that have nothing but sin,
" should lay hold of his righteousness, and wisdom,
" and strength, for I have nothing of my own. My
" spirit is like one at the door, waiting to be called
" in, I could have no access to ask for any thing,
" but that I may go home, and that he would make
" haste, and make no long tarrying.

" I love all that come and feed on his flesh and
" Blood; I feel that he, and not any thing here, is
" my rest and happiness, I love eternity, because he is
" there; I speak with, and cry to him, O the thick-
" ness of this flesh which hides him from me; it is in-
" deed lawful to be weary of it, for it is a thick veil of
" darkness; and I feel clearly, 'tis this, that makes
" me weary of every thing here, and longing to go
" home, to my dear SAVIOUR. O thou who didst
" bleed to death, and who art alive, Come and take
" me home; and as for the passage I have commited
" that to thee, to take care of me; I am thine here,
" and for ever, I am one of thy redeemed, the fruit of
" thy blood and sweat, and thy will is my heaven.

" I feel my spirit continually, as it were, from
" home; and that I am one of the Lamb's company,

N   " and

" and belong to him, and can't be long from him.
" My fpirit cries, LORD, thou canft not be GOD, and
" not pity and love me, — becaufe thou haft given
" me what thou haft promifed in pity, to a poor,
" broken, penitent and humbled fpirit, and alfo faith
" to lay hold of thy righteoufnefs and blood. O LORD
" thou canft not leave me long here, thou muft pity,
" and call me home, for I am a ftranger here. I love
" the glorified fpirits, and long to be among them,
" becaufe they behold his Glory ; and becaufe they
" have no guile, nor deceit, nor felf, nor ftrange
" gods, nor any other corruption, nor wifdom or
" righteoufnefs, but only in the Lamb.

" I find my felf growing very weak, to day ; and
" am in much pain, and feel my fpirit crying, O my
" dear Father, art thou coming, to ftrike the laft
" ftroke ? When our SAVIOUR fhall come and raife
" my fpirit, from nature, and death, and every thing
" here below to his own Spirit ; — then I fhall know
" what it is, to be cleanfed, and purified, I feel, that
" my fpirit goes to GOD, not as his creature, but as
" his Child, and the purchafe of his Blood.

" My dear SAVIOUR, did fhine on me fweetly,
" this afternoon, O let me eat no more, the bread,
" that perifheth, be thou to me, from henceforth,
" my bread, and food forever, be thou to me, my Sun,
" and let me fee this, no more. O hear the cries of
" thy poor worm ; thy Blood, has done the work ;
" take

" take me from this body of clay, for I am here in
" prifon, O take me there, where thou fheweft thy
" Glory, and indulge a worm, fick of love, longing to
" come home I adore thee, for all the graces beftow-
" ed on all the fpirits round the throne; and efpecial'y
" on my own poor fpirit. And as for my concerns
" and cares, I have none but thine, and thou muft
" take care of them, call me hence, and make no long
" tarrying. I cried again, if I am not willing to be
" cloathed with thy righteoufnefs, then do not hear
" me, and if thy Blood does not overbalance all my fins,
" then do not hear me, and if my work is not done,
" 'and if it is not thy will I fhould come home, do not
" hear me, for what am I, a worm before thee. I then
" cried and prayed for the whole race of mankind,
" loving them all, but more efpecially, for this little
" family, which he has given me, intreating him, that
" he would be in the midft of them, and reveal himfelf
" unto them, as crucified before them, and banifh
" every fpirit from them, but his own,

" I faid, I have no name, worthy of preferving, to
" pofterity, but only as far, as it is connected with
" thine, and that, I leave to thee ; I love this body,
" becaufe thou haft made it, and haft united it to
" thyfelf, and I give it to thee, to be embalmed in the
" earth, where thine was laid. I call upon thee, as
" a child does, upon his dear Father ; and I weep over
" all the fin of the world, efpecially, over that fin,
" that thy Blood, and fufferings, are defpifed.

" I feel my fpirit, leaving all places, and men, here
" below,

" below, and going to my Father; and to my native
" country, home; yea my own, home. And tho' I
" am here below, in his kingdom; yet, whilst I wait,
" to be called home, my longings, and cries, are
" infatiable indeed. And, when the LORD of Glory,
" anfwers me, that I fhall foon go to him , my fpirit,
" does fo burn with love, to that dear SAVIOUR, that
" I flee to him, and can take no denial, I can't ftay
" here, and tho I am but a bit of duft, and nothing
" before thee, yet O Father, may I without offending
" thee, afk this one efpecial favour, O SAVIOUR, give
" me leave, tho' a worm, to afk without offending,
" that my time may be fhortened. O my dear LORD,
" I muft love thee, and weep at thy feet, and wreftle
" with thee, till thou appeareft unto me. This, is thy
" lower houfe, and thou art my life, and my all here
" below, that, is thy upper houfe, and thou art gone
" before me, and therefore I muft come. Thou canft
" not leave me long, thou art both here, and there
" alfo, my heaven.

" I muft have the SAVIOUR, indeed, for he, is my all;
" all that others have, in the world, and in religion,
" and in themfelves, I have in thee, pleafures, riches,
" fafety, honor, life, righteoufnefs, holinefs, wifdom,
" blifs, joy, gayety, and happinefs, and by the fame
" rule, that each of thefe, is dear to others, he muft
" be dear to me. And if a child, longs for his father;
" a traveller, for the end of his journey; a workman,
" to finifh his work; a prifoner, for his liberty; an
" heir,

" heir, for the full poffeffion of his eftate ; fo, in
" all thefe refpects, I can't help longing, to go
" home.

" My fpirit rejoices, within me, in feeing, that he
" that made me, will call me hence , and it is indeed
" weary, of all things here, having all kinds of an-
" fwers, and confirmations, from the Holy Spirit, re-
" lating to my approaching departure. Lord, this
" is thy houfe, and not mine, I built it for thee, and
" not for myfelf; and the family I have, in it, is thine.
" For thee I nurfe them ; and the papers, which I
" leave behind me, are written for thee, and not for my
" ufe. And feeing all in this light, I feel, it is eafy to
" part with all ; my fpirit therefore, crieth continually,
" O come, come, Lord come quickly. I feel my
" fpirit, among the fuppliants here, before the throne ;
" and find freedom to fay, I have done my work, I have
" finifhed my teftimony, I have run my race ; what
" more remains for me to do, but to come home, to
" my own dear God, and Father, and Friend, and
" beft relation. All thy friends, are my friends , and
" all thy enemies, are mine. O come, Lord Jesus,
" come quickly, and take me home to reft. I feel
" my fpirit rejoicing and finging,

" *My Lord, is gone, and I muft go,*
" *I cannot ftay content below.*"

Being confin'd by his diforder to his bed, and not
able to write himfelf, he faid, " Blefled be God, my

work

" work is done, and I know that I am going to my
" dear GOD and Father, for he hath my heart, yea
" my whole heart "— Adding, " tho the enemy is
" permitted to torment my body, bleffed be the LORD,
" he is not fuffered to come near my fpirit." He, very
often, joyfully repeated thefe words, " Glory be to
" GOD, death hath no fting ! Death, has loft its
" fting !" And again, he broke out, as one full of
faith and affurance, " It is more clear to me, that
" GOD, is my everlafting Father, and that I fhall go
" to him fcon " He over, and over again, expreffed,
how exceeding dear and precious the SAVIOUR was
to him, and faid, " This is following JESUS. We
" are come to Mount Sion, and I am on Mount
" Sion, I faw great glory before, in that, GOD Man,
" JESUS, but nothing to what I now behold in Him !"
And at another time, when he awoke from a flumber
through the extreme pain of his body, his fpirit leaping
within him, as a prifoner coming to liberty, thinking
this the laft ftroke, he cried out, O JESUS, " here I
" come, here I come to Thee." — Some time afterwards, he expreffed his faith, and longing defires, to
" depart, faying, I am in great pain, but all is well,
" all is well, he hath fettled all things well; O, how
" would it be, if the fting of death, had not been taken
" away. O that I could now go home, for my work
" is done here."

AND, as he conftantly contemplated, on the infinite
fufferings, of the Redeemer; which was always his

pleafant

ant theme, he faid, " I am in great pain, but CHRIST
" by his fufferings hath taken away the fting, of my
" fufferings: O here is victory, indeed, great is the
" Glory, but narrow is the way to it, O how full is the
" world of falfe faith, and falfe hope"— Then, confidering the great faithfulnefs, of the LORD, to him,
he breathed out the language of his foul, in thefe words,
" O the dear Redeemer, he keeps my heart with
" himfelf." —— When he was in the greateft pain,
he often, cried out, " O this cup, Bleffed be GOD
" for this laft cup. JESUS drank it all for me, —
" I fhall be foon with that GOD, that died for me, to
" fave me, to all eternity." And thus, he went
home to Reft, in the LORD. July 21, 1773. In the
60th year, of his age.

MANY more divine fayings, came from him juft
before he departed, which were not taken down,
whereby, he teftified his great love to precious fouls,
and the concern, he was in, about them.

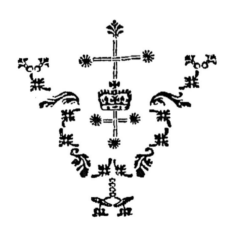

His EPITAPH.

NEAR the Communion Table lie the Remains of
HOWELL HARRIS Esquire.
Born at *Trevecka*, Jan. the 23ᵈ, 1713—14, O S.
Here where his Body lies, he was convinced of sin
Had his pardon Sealed;
And felt the Power of CHRIST's precious Blood,
At the holy Communion.
Having tasted Grace, himself, He resolved to declare to others,
What GOD had done, for his soul.
He was the first Itinerant Preacher of Redemption
In this period of Revival, in *England*, and *Wales*.
He Preached the Gospel,
For the space, of thirty-nine Years
Till He was taken to his final rest.
He received those who sought Salvation
Into his House;
Then sprung up the Family, at *Trevecka*,
To whom he Faithfully ministered, unto his end,
As an indefatigable Servant, of GOD,
And faithful Member, of the Church, of *England*,
His end,
Was more blessed than his beginning,
Looking to JESUS, crucified
He rejoiced, to the last, that Death had lost its sting.
He fell asleep, in JESUS, at *Trevecka*, July 21, 1773,
An now rests blessedly from all his labours.

UNDER the same Stone, lie also, the Remains of his late wife
ANNE HARRIS·
Daughter of JOHN WILLIAMS, of *Skreen*, Esquire.
Who departed this life, March 9ᵗʰ 1770, Aged 58
She, loved the LORD JESUS, relied on his Redeeming
Grace, and Blood, and with her last breath, declared her
Confidence in Him.

They left one beloved Daughter, who was the constant Object of
their Prayers, and care, and honours their venerable Memory.

DAN. xii 3.
*A'r doethion a ddisgleiriant fel disglen deb y ffurfafen; a's rhai a
droant lawer i gyfiawnder a fyddant fel y Ser, byth yn dragywydd*

AN

ELEGIAC POEM

On the Death of

HOWELL HARRIS, Efq;

Who died the 21 of *July*, 1773.

——*All the Congregation mourned for Aaron*——

WHAT penfive, folemn, doleful tidings found ?
All *Sion's Sons*, fhould deeply feel the Wound :
A Brother, Friend, a Father Dear, is gone,
HARRIS is dead his Battle's fought and won.
What Tongue, can tell ? What Hand, can paint the Lofs ?
Of one fo fteady, under JESU's Crofs.

Hail ! happy Soul, thy mourning Days, are o'er;
Thou'lt bear about, a mortal Frame, no more.
No more, fhall Pain, or Anguifh, thee confine,
Or, on a dying Bed, thy Head recline
No more, fhall Sin opprefs, thy righteous Soul;
Nor Grief, come near, while endlefs Ages roll.
No more (when glows thy Heart, with pure Defire)
Thou'lt feel the force, of Perfecution's Fire,

†   No

No more, for calling Sinners, home to God,
Shalt thou be ston'd, 'till ftain'd with thine own Blood;
No more, fhall it be faid, thou wrong'ft the poor,
Or tak ft their wealth, to gain thyfelf a Store,
No more, with what is worfe, fhalt thou be tri'd,
By vain Profeffors, fetting thee afide.

Advanc d, beyond their Frowns, beyond their Praife,
HARRIS with Angels, tunes his grateful Lays.
He fits, with all thofe radiant Hofts, above,
And fwims, in Seas, of pure celeftial Love.
He meets his bleffed *Partner*, gone before,
They join, to praife their God, and part no more.
She, like a brilliant Diamond, appears,
And helps to decorate, the Crown, he wears.
Not her alone, but Thoufands more, there be,
Whom God converted, by his Miniftry.

Ye Moon, and Stars, who make our Ev'ning's Light,
Tell us, how oft, he groan'd to God, by Night?
Say, rifing Sun, yea tell us, dawning Day,
How foon, he left his Bed, to praife and pray.
Say, Walls and Clofets, every fecret Place,
How oft, he fupplicated God, for Grace?
How oft, he with his bleffed LORD, did meet;
And fill'd with Love, bow'd, at his facred Feet.
Say, thou infernal Prince, how thou didft rage,
When HARRIS, did againft thy Caufe engage,
And let thine Emiffaries here, proclaim,
How, mov'd by thee, they vilifi'd his Name.

Say, ye bleſt Angels, how, diſpatch'd from GOD,
To guard him, round on every ſide, ye ſtood.
Say Sinners, ſay, how oft, with warm Deſire,
He warn d you to eſcape, eternal Fire ?

Let Towns, and Streets, Houſes, and Fields proclaim,
How zealouſly, he did the Faith maintain.
Then let each Chriſtian, with a ſecret Sigh,
Reverberate, TREVECKA's penſive Cry.
Let every Heart, lift up a fervent Pray'r,
That old *Elijah*'s Mantle, may be there.
That GOD, from Age, to Age, may carry on,
The work which He, thro' HARRIS, hath begun,
That all, who ſhall that Saint of GOD ſucceed,
Like him, may prove, true *Iſraelites* indeed.

How glorioufly he ſhines; What mean theſe Sighs ?
Why flow theſe torrents, from our languid Eyes ?
But Ah ! we weep, that he from us ſhould part,
Who ſo minutely, trac'd the Sinner's Heart.
Who all the Reaſonings therein diſclos'd,
And all the Devil's Stratagem's, expos'd.
The Man, whom GOD, hath raiſed (in his Youth)
In *Wales*, to propagate the Goſpel truth
He ſet his Brow, as Braſs, no Fleſh he fear'd,
Eſſential truth, he faithfully declar'd.
His Grace, and Knowledge, Numbers to him drew,
They to his Houſe, like Doves, to Windows flew.

[❋]

He caufed Thoufands, by the Pow'r of GOD,
To part with Sin, and flee to JESU's Blood.
He fpake, nor did his Works, his Words deny,
He liv'd each Day, as tho' that Night he'd die.

Not all the Pow'rs of Hell, could *him* difmay,
He, to the end, purfu'd the narrow Way.
The Paths of Peace, inceffantly he trod,
Then, died exulting, in his SAVIOUR GOD.
His Spirit, catholic, was Friend, to all;
Who JESU's Image bore, who on Him call.
A mighty Conqu'ror, as thro' life, in Death,
Still fhouting Vict'ry with his lateft Breath.
And tho' his Body fuffer'd, grievous Smart,
He faid, " The Dear Redeemer, keeps my Heart."

And when the great I AM, fhall roll the Skies,
And bid unnumber'd Worlds, to Judgment rife!
Then HARRIS, by his Lord, fhall be confeft,
And Soul, and Body, enter into Reft.
Return triumphant, to his deftin'd Throne,
And dwell with GOD, in extafies, unknown.

F I N I S.

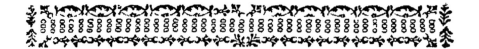

HIS
LETTERS.

LETTER I.

To Mr. H———— G————.

Trevecka, Oct. 24, 1738.

Dear Christian Friend,

I Received your favoury Letter, laft Night; in which, you make me fee, a caufe for trembling, and blufhing, in afking the advice, and prayer, of one, fo unfit, for both. Oh that we could think of ourfelves, and others, as we realy are, vile, and blind creatures. Oh that GOD would empty us of our felves, and fill us with clearer fight, and nobler Ideas of his dear SON; how little would every thing appear to us then! How fweet would revilings found in our ears, while our Eyes would be fixed, on JESUS Crucified. What are we that we fhould be counted worthy to fuffer for his fake? Surely this is an honor, which is above the reach of the carnal world, which the KING of Heaven confers but upon few. Oh how humbly then fhould we lie at his feet, admiring his free Electing Love, if in the leaft he diftinguifhes fuch poor, vile, worms as we are; Surely none ftands in need of the prayers of prevailing Saints as much as

I do; therefore I defire that you would ftrive for me, that I may gain the conqueft over felf, my grand enemy. That I may lay lower at my SAVIOUR's feet, accounting it my greateft honor, if I fhould be thought worthy, to be reviled for his fake.

I hope, you are admitted, to have fome cherifhing fmiles from JESUS, thefe, will fweeten every afflidtion, temperate all croffes, and feafon all the bittereft portions to us. Our dear SAVIOUR is never dearer than when the battle is hotteft. When enemies frown, ridicule and threaten, O then, when the foul is humbled, the old man trampled under foot, and faith kept in clofe exercife, how fweet is the private affociating of fincere Chriftian Soldiers who join together to fend up hearty cries, at the throne of Grace? To have a frefh fight of the Captain, will animate fainting Souls —— O that we were laid low enough in the duft, and truly unbottomed of felf, then could enemies without be of little hinderance to us — But the great, and willing Captain of Salvation, knows beft how to marfhal his army; and excercife his Soldiers. What we need examine moft carefully, is, whether we are realy, and entirely his, I find a moft deceitful heart, within me, now owning him, and promifing great things, but which on trial will fail, or betray me. I hope the main bufinefs of our aquaintance, at home, and abroad, fhall be to no other end, but to encourage, caution, and try each other, that at laft, we may meet with

the

the reſt of the LORD's faithful ſervants, in the regions above. Sure, there are rewards enough, to make amends, in a few moments, for the labours, fatigues, croſſes, perſecutions, and troubles, of many ages, ſpent here Let us hold on our way then, ſince we are aſſured, we have ſuch a Captain, who will never leave us. And being alſo aſſured, our labours are not in vain in the LORD. Oh, how greatly doth my Soul rejoice, that GOD ſhould own you, in ſuch a particular manner, as to make your houſe, his palace for feeding his little ones, and your ſelf, a father, to the babes, now left to the jaws of lions, were it not for an inviſible hand. I hope you will by no means drop it, if you reap any benefit by meeting together, for fear of that poor worm, *Man*, ſince his Maſter is confined in chains. I rather fear, the policy of Satan's working on the inward man, *&c.* Pray think, when you meet in future, of the poor little flock hereabouts, and receive the ſincere love, and moſt affectionate wiſhes, of

Your ſincere friend, in CHRIST,

H. H.

PLEASE to preſent my ſincere Reſpects to your Spouſe and Family.

LETTER II.

To Mr. M——P——, in Briſtol.

Trevecka, Nov. 21, 1738.

Dear Brother in Chriſt,

I Am ſo hurried about, that I can hardly ſpare time, according to my wiſh to correſpond with

O 2

my

my deareſt friends. But now I have ſtolen a few
minutes to ſend you this Letter, and wiſh that it may
meet you near the Gates of the new Jeruſalem,
raviſhed with the ſight of Jesu's infinite love, O that
we could aim more at his Glory, here below — having our eyes, and ears, ſhut, to the things of the world
and the fleſh Oh that we had more of his humble,
ſincere, loving, and innocent ſpirit and nature, and
that we could keep more cloſe to him, ſo that we
ſhould know more of him, and be kept more tenderly
affected towards his people; and be more humbly,
and prudently zealous, and ſpiritually bold, to ſtand up
for him, againſt the raging villains, and torrents of ſin.
Pray let us ſtrengthen each other, againſt this villain
and enemy of ſouls, *Self*. So likewiſe, let us mutually
aſſiſt each other, to ſtir up our drawſy ſpirits, ſo to
talk, think of, and ſpeak to this glorious Prince of
peace, as is becoming us, towards ſo faithful, tender,
loving, condeſcending, and merciful a God and Redeemer. Let us not only act as moral men and gen-
tiles, but by our meek, and innocent behaviours, and
mortifications, let us alſo convince the world, that we
have realy our affections ſet on things above. *Col* iii.
1, 2, 5, 13. Oh that we were all love, to this dear
Jesus and alſo more heavenly, more on the wings
of faith, and leſs on the ground; all our converſation
ſhould be in heaven, for there, is our dear Jesus.
Oh let us not delight in any thing, or place, wherein we may not hope, to meet our ſweet Lord, Oh
that we may know him more, then would our hearts be

drawn

drawn into more ardent defires after him, we fhould be more lively, and vigorous, to labour for him, and more chearful to fuffer, and undergo all the hardfhips we fhould meet with in following him : What would fufferings, ridicule, loffes, hunger, and even death it felf be, while his Spirit affifteth us ? when you are drawn neareft to the Throne, or go into the prefence Chamber, I beg you would think of me, as one that am very ignorant of the word of GOD, and very negligent — and I fear, never have learnt well, to be quite unbottomed of felf — nor am I yet able to do all clearly to the Glory of him, to whom all the Glory is due. But my dear Redeemer has done wonderfully for me — yet I find it very difficult to come from under the covenant of works, to that of Grace, but this is yet within his power to accomplifh or bring about. I have had fome benefit from reading the *Sincere Convert, and Bunyan's Law and Grace.* I find Satan by a fpirit of Bigotry in all parties, as well as with us, has affected to do great mifchief, in many places among CHRIST s little flock, to embitter their fpirit, againft others, of a different parfuafion, and diverting their thoughts, from the fubftance, to the fhadow, of religion. Oh how fhould our fouls rejoice, that our days, are reforming days, there is a hopeful profpect, in fome places, that would rejoice your Soul ; we have feveral Societies, in this and other Counties, of young people, meeting together to pray, and converfe, &c. which are hopeful, fome are of a year's ftanding, and fome more,

The

The Clergy have oppofed us, but GOD hath awak-ened fome, and made them able Minifters of his truth.

YOU have heard of the Rev. Mr *Griffith Jones* of Carmarthenfhire, and the Rev. M^r. *Rowlands*, of Cardiganfhire, and fome other Clergymen in this County, who preach CHRIST powerfully, there is alfo in thefe parts, a Baptift preacher, that GOD has owned very much, together with fome other Diffenting Minifters.

THUS, I have given you a hint, how our King's intereft profpers in *Wales* O pray heartily in private, and public, that conviction, may end in true conver-fion, and that we fhould not reft, till we have a faving knowledge of JESUS CHRIST, and increafe, in all the increafe of GOD.

> I am your moft
>
> affectionate, hearty well wifher ;
>
> H. H.

LETTER III.

The following is a Copy of Mr. G—— Whitfield's firft Letter to Mr. H——H.

London Dec. 20th, 1738.

My dear Brother,

THo' I am unknown to you, in perfon, yet I have long been united to you in fpirit, and have been rejoiced to hear, how the good pleafure of the LORD, profpered, in your hands — Go on my dear Brother, go on, be ftrong in the LORD, and in the

power

power of his might, and the Spirit of CHRIST, and of Glory, shall rest upon you, most effectually: which has, and still, is opening doors before you, for preaching the everlasting Gospel. There have been, and will be, many adversaries; yet be not afraid, He that sent you will assist, comfort, and protect you, and make you more than conquerour, thro' his great love. I am a living monument, of this truth; for the Divine strength, has been often magnified, in my weakness. I have tasted, that the LORD is gracious, I have felt his power, and from mine own expereince, can say, that in doing, or suffering the will of JESUS CHRIST, there is great reward. Blessed be his holy name, there seems to be a great pouring out of the Spirit, at *London*, and we walk in the comfort of the HOLY Ghost, and are edified. You see my dear Brother, the freedom I have taken, in writing to you, if you would favour me, with a line, or two, by way of answer, you would greatly rejoice, both me, and many others; why, should not we tell one another, what GOD has done, for our Souls? My dear Brother, I love you, in the bowels of JESUS CHRIST, and wish you may be the spiritual Father of thousands, and shine as the Sun, in the firmament, in the kingdom, of your heavenly Father. My hearty love, to M^r. *Jone* ; Oh how shall I joy to meet you, at the Judgment seat of CHRIST. How you would honor me, if you would send a line to, dear Brother,

  Your affectionate, tho'
    unworthy Brother, in CHRIST,
      G. W.

LETTER IV.

*Mr. H—— H. Anſwer to the Fore-going Letter of the
Rev. Mr. G—— W.*

Glamorgan Jan. 8ᵗʰ, 1739.

Dear Brother,

I Was moſt agreeably ſurpriſed, laſt Night, by a
Letter from you, of the 20ᵗʰ paſt, the Character you bear, the ſpirit that I ſee, and feel, in your
work, and the cloſe union of my Soul, and ſpirit, to
yours, will not allow me to uſe any apology, in my
return to you. Though this is the firſt time of
our correſpondance ; yet I can aſſure you, I am no
ſtranger to you ; when I firſt heard of you, and
your labours, and ſuccefs, my Soul was united to
you, and engaged to ſend addreſſes to heaven, on your
behalf ; when I read your Diary, I had ſome uncommon Influence, of the Divine preſence, ſhining on
my poor Soul, almoſt continually. And my Soul,
was in an uncommon manner, drawn out on your
account, — but I little thought, our good LORD, and
Maſter intended I ſhould ever ſee your hand writing. I hope we ſhall be taught more, and more, to
admire, the wonderful goodneſs of GOD : in his acts
of free Grace ; ſure no perſon is under ſuch obli-
gations, to advance the Glory, of his free goodneſs,
and Grace, as this poor prodigal. But alas, how
little ſenſe have I in my Soul, of all his wonderful
bleſſings ! pray for me, that I may find my heart,
more drawn out, in love, and praiſe, to him. Oh
how raviſhing is it, to hear, of ſuch demonſtrations

of

of the divine love, and favour, to *London!* and to make your joy, greater still, I have some more good news to send you from *Wales.* There is a great revival in Cardiganshire, thro' one Mr. *D. Rowlands,* a Church Clergyman, and he has been much owned and blessed in Caermarthenshire also —— We have also a sweet prospect in Breconshire, and part of Monmouthshire; and in this County, where I am now, the revival prospers, there is also here a young Dissenting Minister of much use, who also is a man of universal charity — There is such another in Montgomryshire — I have been twice there, and there seems to be some shining beams of the Gospel of grace —— There are two or three young Curates in Glamorganshire (where now I am) that are well wishers to religion — and we have one exceeding sweet, and valuable man, with us in Breconshire; but enemies are many, and powerful; therefore I beg the help of your prayers, and the prayers, of all your bretheren, that GOD would stand up for his cause, and interest, against all his visible, and invisible, enemies.

I hint this, in general, as I could not testify my love, any way more agreeably to your soul, than to let you know, how the interest of our good, gracious, and dear SAVIOUR JESUS CHRIST, prospers here-abouts. Oh! that I had more love, in my soul, more humble zeal, and spiritual boldness. Surely I should blush to think, the name of such an igno-

P   rant,

rant, negligent, and unprofitable fervant, fhould reach your ears. I rejoice on the one fide, and fear on the other, by reafon of the relicts of felf, pride, &c. which I find, are not quite dead within. I would blefs GOD, that inclined you to write to me, and efpecially, for making your Letter fo favoury to my fainting foul. Oh ! that we could do more, for fo loving a Mafter —— that his very enemies, by feeing our innocent behaviour, and fruitfulnefs, and love, &c. may be brought to glorify the Redeemer, and to think well of his ways, &c. I am in a great hurry, as I am called away to difcourfe now quickly, yet I could not drop this opportunity without obliging you — and were you to come to *Wales*, I hope, it would not be labour in vain —— but I leave this to him that knows beft how to difpofe of us ; I hope the faithful account I have given you, of the benefit I have received from you, will excite you to fend again, a line to him, that would be, fincerely

> Yours, in CHRIST JESUS, whilft
>
> *H. H.*

LETTER V.

To a Sifter *in* Monmouthfhire.

Nov. 30th, 1739.

Dear Sifter,

I Hope, our dear LORD, is breathing his fweet, pure, and gentle mind, into your foul, and is drawing you up to himfelf. O ! Eternity, eternity !

make

make all fure, for the dying hour is coming on. See whether you daily, and hourly, feel fresh life coming from the Head, JESUS CHRIST. You cannot bear fruit, except you abide in the Vine. See then, that nothing obstruct the current of virtue, flowing from the Vine, to you the Branch. Cherish the believing frame, and fee, that every thing fends you out of your felf, and from the creatures, and ordinances, to him, in whom all fulnefs dwells. Beware of false hopes; fee, that you reft not, in any thing you have attained to, but feek for more confidence in your dear LORD. When all friends fail, yet *He changeth not.* O, try his faithfulnefs, if he hides himfelf, it is to try your confidence in him. Therefore be not difcouraged, at inward, or outward, dark threatening clouds. And if you are feemingly deferted of all, and quite forgotten, this is only to deftroy an enemy, that keeps you from enjoying your beft Friend. I know not how to communicate comfort to you, under your prefent outward trials — but beware of common reafoning, flee to CHRIST, afk, and and follow his advice; rely, and live on his promife, wait patiently, all is in his hands, it fhall be for your good. It is to make you dead to vifible things, that you may enjoy more of him, whom the world knows nothing of. Our eternal happinefs is begun, if the kingdom of heaven is within us. Pray look to the growth of your faith, and fee, leaft even a fight of your corruption (which ought to humble you deeply, and to make deep impreffions of godly forrow)

fhould

fhould feed unbelief. Beware of doubts, and reafon-ings, when it is dark, dead, and hard, when you can fee nothing but fin, then, run to CHRIST, fo much the fafter, and you fhall find him full of grace and truth, faithful is he that promifed; therefore, put all your truft, and confidence in him.

I hope the LORD fent me, to the places I vifitted, fince I left you, therefore, beg for a heart to blefs the glorious JEHOVAH, in CHRIST, on my ac-count. I hope, the LORD owned me at St. *Andrew's*, and St. *Nicholas*, to put a ftop to the growing *Ar-minian* errors effectually — Yefterday I difcourfed in *Cowbridge* market-houfe, and was a little interrupt-ed. After I had done difcourfing, I had private con-verfation with five leading men in town, and I hope it was to purpofe, and that the LORD will fend me there again. I am now in my way to *Pembroke-fhire*, I loft my way on the hills laft night —— but the LORD remembered his covenant. Sin often re-bels in me, but faith in CHRIST's death, daily mor-tifies, and fubdues it, and my foul is fet at liberty. Bleffed be GOD, who is as good to let us have ferious impreffions of death fet home on our fouls, to quicken us to diligence, to make our calling ond election fure. 2 *Pet* i. 10. O! beg for clearer evidences, ftrong feal-ings, more evident witneffes of the Spirit of GOD. Be ftill crying, LORD fearch, and try me, and fhew me more, and more, in a clearer light, that thou haft loved me, with an everlafting love; and that none

fhall

fhall pluck me out of thy hand. Continue pleading, that you may be more like him, that you may
more furely fay, he is yours. fo that if a drawn
fword fhould be prefented to your breaft, it might not
furprife you in the leaft; becaufe that you had been
affured, on a folid and right ground.

I am yours in CHRIST,

H. H.

LETTER VI.

To Mifs M——— Llwyngwarren.

Rhos-Tywarch, Dec. 10th, 1740.

Dear Madam,

WHen you are fully convinced, of my end, in
writing to you, you will not be furprifed at
it, Eternity is at the door. Our Hearts are full of
Devices, the world is full of Temptations, and all our
nature is corrupt, and draws us from GOD. GOD's
Spirit may eafily, in his firft working upon us, be
grieved, and quenched, and if he once leaves us, we
fall to hardnefs, and carelefnefs, and indifference,
which is the moft dreadful condition we can be in:
For thefe reafons, I could not help writing, to cherifh
thofe good defires, already feen in you, and O!
that this may find you looking up to JESUS, and
comforted with his love; being made quite willing,
to renounce all for him, feeing yourfelf quite loft,
without him, feeing him of more value, than ten
thoufand worlds. If you fall fhort of him, and will
not be fully united to him, how dreadful will death,

and

and eternity be? What will a good name, Blood, beauty, riches, friends and relations, avail us then? O dear Madam, there is an earnest prayer set on my heart for you, *Rom* xvi. 1. to see you born again. Be not surprised, I tell you, that you must see yourself, the greatest of sinners; even on the same footing with harlots—for we are all such in heart, though restrained in the outward man. Pray rest not, till you know, your sins are forgiven. What comfort is there, in any thing, till we enjoy this? ask it with all your heart, and you shall have it.

SHALL you shine with *Abraham*, *Isaac* and *Jacob*, when our dear LORD will come, on the firmament, to be glorified in his saints, and in all those that now, can see that day, with an eye of faith, and renounce all for him, and choose affliction with his people, rather than enjoy all the pleasures of sin for a moment? *Heb* xi. 25. O look up, to your heavenly FATHER's house, and you will soon quit earthly joys. Pray give not your eyes to slumber, nor the temples of your head to take any rest, till you feel CHRIST in you, and you in him. O pray for that broken heart, it is GOD's gift, ask it, and you shall have it, reason not about it, but still run to CHRIST. If you feel your heart hard, and cannot taste his love, and cannot lay a thing home to heart, as you would wish, let not that discourage you from going, but let it make you go the more confidently to CHRIST.

In

In him you will find ftrength when you are weak,
light when you are dark, life when you are dead,
love when you are cold, comfort when you are dejected, a Friend at all times, and a remedy for all
fpiritual difeafes. O let nothing fhare your heart
with him, he is willing to take you, as you are, a
a poor, blind, weak, loft, helplefs worm. *Rev.* iii 18.
If you are made willing to part with the right eye,
right arm, and all for him but if he fhall not have
all your heart, he will not take any part of it, if
you will not be wholly united to him, all your fins
will meet upon your own head, and condemn you,
in the laft day, and all the phials of God's wrath,
will be poured upon you: O ! the thought of it is
moft dreadful, and ftrikingly awful ! Halt not then
between two minds ! Let either God, or the world
and the flefh, have you all. O that I could go with
you in my arms, to our dear Jesus ! there I long
to fee you, but you muft firft, wear the crown of
thorns, before you are crowned with glory. you
muft fuffer croffes, and perfecutions with Christ,
before you fhall reign with him . fit down now, and
caft up the coft. Beware of refolving, in your own
ftrength; that is building on the fand, and it will
fall. You muft receive Christ, and then build
on him, and your building fhall ftand. I fhall, according to the power given me, endeavour to think
of you ; and I fhall hope foon to hear you fay, that
you know, that your Redeemer liveth, and that your
fins are all forgiven. Concern for your foul, would
make

make it defireable, to have a line; to let me know how it is with you, in the inward man. May the LORD guide, and lead you into all truth.

I am yours,

Cordially in our dear LORD,

H. H.

LETTER VII.

To Mr. T——, Panchefton

Manachlog, Dec. 10th, 1740.

Dear Brother,

I Could not let flip this opportunity, without fending you my hearty wifhes, for your growth in knowledge of the myfteries of GOD's kingdom of grace in the heart, and may the Spirit of light, and power, always reft upon you. You have many enemies to encounter, but none fo dangerous as felf, and unbelief, with their infeparable companions; confulting with flefh and blood, fearing man, doubting the faithfulnefs of the moft faithful Friend, &c. O, how fhould we dread felf-love, felf-righteoufnefs, felf-will, felf-confidence, and felf-wifdom! all thefe, if not deftroyed, oppofe the fetting up of CHRIST's kingdom, in our fouls, and tempt us to deny him, and they have each of them, their armour to defend themfelves, carnal-reafonings, and all that are born after the flefh, with all their preaching, and converfation defend them. O my dear Brother; in a teacher, that is not receiving from the Spirit of GOD, nothing is more dangerous than letter-learning, and

head

head, or book-knowledge. It would be well, if we knew, and preached, no more than we felt, and were willing, to be fools, till CHRIST makes us wife , then we fhould be wife indeed. Whatever you may fuffer, from the blind leaders of the blind, who are a curfe to the nation, let me beg you, as I long to fee you fhine, with the faithful at laft , be ftrong in faith, and fear not. Then, fhall the Spirit of glory reft upon you, and you fhall have ftrength, according to your day : I am an inftance and a witnefs of this. My moft ardent wifhes, and prayers are, that you may be made faithfull. I fee, we ftand in continual need of the Spirit of GOD, to wound, and heal us, to caft us down, and lift us up, to fhew us our mifery, and help us to deftroy fin ; to work grace, and to act with grace, when wrought in us ; and to make, and keep us nothing, in our own eyes : nothing lefs than Almighty power, can do this well. But a fight of forgiving love, and a juftifying JESUS, can make us leave all our idols, and love him, with all our hearts, and fouls. How can we love him, if we are not perfuaded he loves us ? Faith, is the fpring of every grace, and all true obedience. And unbelief is the root, or fountain-head, of all rebelion, and difobedience, and feeds every luft. I fee but few convinced of the evil, or of the fin of unbelief, though it makes GOD a liar, and denies all his glorious perfections, renders the word of GOD, praying, converfing, &c. of no effect, bars the heart againft CHRIST, blinds the mind, deftroys the love, eftranges

Q

us from God; and feeds self-love, lust, slavish fear, love of the world, &c And if any, but surely much of it remains in the saints, And O! how does it dishonor God, stop their growth in grace, and give Satan the advantage over them. And most think, that to doubt (which is the fruit of unbelief) is to be on sure footing whereas, all ought to be assured, that they are either out of Christ, or in Christ. Most think to go towards heaven by doing, and not by believing, working for life, and not from life received, with Christ in the head, and self in the heart. It is in vain to press to holiness, till the root of holiness be in us, which is faith · we cannot grow in sanctification when we are not in a state of justification, and then we press on, to make our calling, and election sure God commands this, and to fear, is yielding to unbelief, least a promise being made, we fall short of it——I know, dear Brother, you will not misconstrue my freedom in this—for love constrains—Write to, and pray for,

Your unworthy Brother,

H. H.

LETTER VIII.

To Mr. M——, Llwyngwarren.

Rhos Tywarch, Dec. — 1740.

Dear Sir,

THE kind reception met with at your house, calls for a return of gratitude, from me. How does it rejoice my soul, that though not many mighty are

called

called and chofen, yet there are fome that dare own
a perfecuted JESUS——He will reward all well, that
can now renounce all for him; *Mofes*, and *Abraham*
knew this well, when the one fhould leave the king's
palace, and the other his native country to obey his
call He is now, as valuable, in the eyes of all that
have the light of faith, to know him, and their mifery
without him. With what joy, fhall I meet you, before his throne, faying to him, LORD, here I am,
and the children which thou haft given me. I know
we fhall be enabled to overcome our fpiritual enemies. The way is very narrow, and it is few (few
indeed, in your ftation) that find it. O, how many
ways has Satan, to make us reft, before we come to
CHRIST. It is dangerous to fpeak peace, when there
is no peace. We muft mourn, before we can be comforted, be wounded, before we can be healed, know
we are blind, before we afk for fight, naked before
we are clothed, poor, before we be made rich, loft,
before we are faved, weak, before we feek ftrength,
renounce all, before we have all , be thirfty, before
we drink of the Water of life, go out from ourfelves,
and the creatures before we come to CHRIST. It
is good to be made fober, meek, and humble, &c.
but morality is not Chriftianity, and outward reformation only, will not do — It is no common thing to
be a Chriftian indeed — we muft be born of GOD,
we muft have a new heart, and have CHRIST formed in us, and feel the power of CHRIST's death,
mortifying the mind, and motions of fins, and the

Q 2   very

very defires, after creatures; find the power of his refurrection, raifing us up from the death of fin, to the
life of righteoufnefs, to live a life of faith, hid with
CHRIST in GOD, whatfoever is fhort of this inward
vital union with CHRIST JESUS, is but delufion.
We may feek wrong, and fo not enter; *Luc* XIII. 24.
We muft ftrive, yea, we may be convinced, and not
converted; we may have reftraining, and not faving grace, we may build, and yet not on the Rock;
we may cleave to the commandments, yet not forfake
all, for CHRIST, as the young man in the gofpel;
Mat. XIX. we may believe in the heart, in fome fenfe,
but not confefs him with the mouth, for fear of man.
Becaufe we love the praife of men, as the *Jews* did, to
whom our LORD and SAVIOUR faid, "How can you
(favingly) believe, that receive praife from one another?" We may be Virgins, and not wife ones; we
may have Lamps, *viz.* light, and knowledge, good
works, obedience, *&c.* and not Oil in the veffels, *viz.*
an inward principle of faith, and love--and CHRIST
at laft hear fay, *I know you not.* We may tremble with
Felix, have another heart with *Saul* the king, be almoft a Chriftian, with *Agrippa,* and yet fall fhort;
we may be made in meafure, *partakers of the* HOLY
GHOST, *and the power of the world to come,* &c. *Heb.*
VII. and be utterly loft, at laft, to all eternity ———

O, Dear Sir! the freedom of fpirit, and mouth, that
I had, when I was in your houfe, makes me believe
you will take it kindly, that love to GOD, and love

to your foul, made me, in the fimplicity of my heart, and a longing defire that you might fhine in glory. Therefore, let me beg of you, not to reft in feeking, till you find, in knocking, till it is opened to you. Reft not till you find CHRIST, and him crucified, till you feel the love of CHRIST conftraining you, and till you fee, and count all things but dung and drofs, for the excellency of the knowledge of the riches of grace, that are laid up, as a hidden treafure in CHRIST, for all, whoever will fo believe in him, as to renounce all for him, the Pearl of great price. Let your dear Daughter draw many, to the miniftry of dear Mr. *Thos.* of *Penchefton* — Beware of fitting under the miniftry of dead, blind guides beware of confultations with flefh and blood — was I there, I would go many times to him; as I could not expect to meet GOD, while I would, on any account whatfoever, neglect powerful means. Heart-fearching minifters are very fcarce, and highly to be had in efteem, for their works fake — The greateft honor we poor mortals can be capable of, is to be perfecuted, for righteoufnefs fake. O, what a favour is it to be reproached for CHRIST's fake! O let us look through vifibles, to that within the vail, and then all fublunaries, will lofe their glory.

DEAR SIR, How do I long to find your houfe become a houfe of prayer, and every member of it a member of CHRIST. O, ftand up for the finking caufe of a glorious LORD, the Mighty JEHOVAH; thofe
that

that will honor him, he will honor them; I cannot help, recommending him, but O how does he
love his caufe ! his glory, comes from it continually—
it is an honor to be in the meaneft office in his houfe.
O that we may hear his voice within us, faying, *Well
done, thou good and faithful fervant, Enter thou into the
joy of thy Lord*—This is more than to be made kings,
and conquerors in the world—With my fincere
refpect, to your dear fpoufe, and all the young ones,

I remain moft affectionately

Yours, in our Dear LORD,

H. H.

L E T T E R IX.

Jan. 30th, 1741.

Dear Friend,

YOURS I received; and return you abundant
thanks, for your great kindnefs towards me,
who am the moft unworthy, and leaft of all Chrift-
ians. O ! for ftrength, and grace, there is none
but GOD alone knows, what heavy burdens are
laid upon poor me, fo that I often cry, *My foul
is exceeding forrowful, even to death.* I have been,
fince I left you, in the very field of battle, within,
and without. I feel my body weak, and my fpirit
grieved, becaufe of fin, in myfelf, and the wickednefs
that is in the world. But though Satan, and his inftruments are mighty; yet, my GOD IS ALMIGHTY,
and I can fay, I am not my own. O, free grace !

I think

I think, we fhould be loft in the proper meditation of it. What can I fay? O, the diftinguifhing love of GOD! O, what amazing, and aftonifhing grace! and fympathizing mercy, to fuch a worm as I, nay, worfe than any worms, for they don't fin, but I do; and yet, blind, and black as I am, my dear LORD loves and pities me. O! the height, depth, and length of his grace! I hear him whifper, to my foul, faying, *I will never leave thee, nor forfake thee* Rejoice thou, O my foul, and blefs GOD for croffes, and trials — for, there is an eternal weight of glory, referved for thee. O, furely, that will be enough, to make amends, for this little affl ction here. O, when fhall I reach my everlafting home! Indeed, I believe, it is but a little while, and I fhall be at home. Sometimes, I feel fuch decay, and fuch bodily weaknefs, that I think it impoffible for me to hold out long. O, join with me! and pray, LORD JESUS, come quickly — But O, what am I? vile duft and afhes — Teach, and make me, O LORD be refigned unto thy heavenly will: and may thy will be my will. Amen.

H H.

LETTER X.

To Mr. A———.

Little Summerford, Oct. 8th, 1741.

Dear Brother,

HOW fweet and lovely is our dear JESUS! all his precious names, and gracious offices, are fuited to all our various and numerous, wants — O,

the

the wifdom of the Divine fcheme of our falvation!
What a fuitable Phyfician, he is to all our maladies!
What a healing virtue is found in his precious
Blood! what an irrefiftible power has the Efficacy
of his Blood, when it is applied to our fouls! How
does it deftroy the power of fin, and Satan! What a
faithful Friend is he, loving us with an everlafting,
unchangeable love! O, what an Almighty Conqueror is he, as a King! never loofing the day, as a
Captain! How tender, loving, and fympathizing,
as an Hufband! How prevalent, as an Interceffor!
How glorious, as a Prieft! purchafing an eternal
peace, pardon, and reft! O, that I could fet forth his
lovelinefs — How terribly black muft unbelief appear
to be, in the eyes of all that he enlightens! as it dif-
honors all his glorious perfections. it makes him
imperfect in all his Offices, unable to fave to the
uttermoft! as a Phyfician not able to heal entirely!
as King, not able to fubdue the enemies of his
Church; as a Friend, unfaithful to his word; and
like us, changing creatures, promifing great things,
and never intending to fulfil them. As a Captain,
not able to conquer or win the day, as a Hufband,
not mindful of his fpoufe; regardlefs of her mifery,
and deaf to her cries, &c. O how much do we de-
ferve ten thoufand hells, for the difhonor we have
done to the SAVIOUR! I fear, there is too little la-
menting, for the evil of the fin of unbelief: If a man
was to fall into whoredom, or drunkennefs, it would
be reckoned a horrid crime, but to live under the

power

power of unbelief, is not much dreaded or ftrove againft. My dear Brother, Pray for power to bear your Teftimony againft this terrible enemy of CHRIST, and our fouls ! Without faith, it had been as well for us (I fee) if CHRIST had not died. O penetrating faith ! What glorious things, does thine eye difcover ! and what glad tidings do we hear, through thy bleffed ear ! and with what Manna, and marrow, and fatnefs, is thy mouth filled, when it is once opened ! How then fhould we take care to nourifh this child, when it is begotten in the heart, even before it is brought-forth into the world of liberty ; to be continually beholding the glory of GOD, in the face of JESUS CHRIST, or till the SUN of Righteoufnefs, fhall fully rife on our fouls. Let us look towards him, in whom dwelleth all the fulnefs of the Godhead bodily ! who is our all in all. As far as faith is in exercife, looking to him, fo far, I rejoice, that I am in the way; fo far as fin has no dominion over me, fo far Satan is evidently bruifed under my feet ; and fo long is the New Creature fed. But when I forget my dear LORD, and forget to look up, and become conceitedly wife again, then I am fliding out of the way, not abiding in his wounds ; then I fall into darknefs, and heavinefs, and confufion, and into the power of the enemy, &c. and I bear no good fruit. But while faith is looking up, and I abide in his love, I am happy. O ! what a terrible doctrine it is to fay, that we muft not have faith in exercife continually ? it is no other than to fay, We

R　　　　　　　　　　　muft

must not receive grace, and bear fruit continually, for CHRIST; but now and then, to ourselves and Satan. But if fo, we must be under the Law, and the power of fin, as long as we live. But, furely this is not the right way, therefore, we must bear our fhield continually, by exercifing our faith, *Eph.* vi. 12, 16, 17, 18.

DEAR Brother, watch over the little Lambs; I am perfuaded, fome of them, belong to our dear LORD. If you pleafe, read this to them, with my kind love to them all, hoping to hear, of their growth in the LORD, and that they begin to know, and love him more, and more, in all his Names, Offices, and Relations, &c. O, that they may never reft, till they know, at all times, that he is their righteoufnefs, and eternal falvation: and not to reft on what they have attained to, but to keep the eye of faith fixed, on the power, fulnefs, faithfulnefs, and watchfulnefs that is in CHRIST — O, may we never reft, till an abiding fenfe of our own vilenefs, ignorance, and helpleffnefs, abides in us, to make us continually look up, where our ftrength, our glory, and grace is laid up, drinking every moment of his fullnefs.

Yours in ours,

H. H.

LETTER

LETTER XI.

To Mrs. S——.

Nov. 12*th*, 1741.

Dear Mrs. S——,

O How does the humble and poor foul thrive? Do you feel you are united to CHRIST? And doth the life that is in him, flow to your dear foul? Are you hungering, and thirfting for this, and continually longing for his abiding prefence with you? Dear Sifter, bear with me, it is out of godly jealoufy I entreat you, to fee narrowly, whether there be no Idols in your heart, any thing nearer than CHRIST. I beg of GOD, to fearch you, leaft after much feeking, you may not find; becaufe you did not feek, with all your heart. Before there can be a marriage, between him and our fouls, there muft be an eternal feparation made between us, and not only the gaiety, and pride, and pomp, and outward conformity to, and pleafures of this evil world—but alfo between us, and the inward defire, after the praife, or good opinion, of any one of our fellow creatures, or after any treafure, or creature-enjoyment; yea, more than that, there muft be a thorough feparation, between us and ourfelves, before we can be truly united to him. We muft come out of our own willing, and reafoning, to GOD; we muft ceafe living to that great Idol, felf; that we may live to him, who died for us, felf muft be fubdued, and CHRIST muft be

exalted,

exalted, and fet up in our fouls, or we cannot be faved. If we live after the flefh, or after the defire and will of the flefh, or nature, we fhall moft certainly perifh, if we carry on an intereft contrary to, or feparate from our LORD's intereft. We are declared to be married to CHRIST, for by faith CHRIST makes himfelf, and us one, and if CHRIST, and all his righteoufnefs and graces are become ours, then it cannot be, but all we have, and are, and can do, are his. We no longer look on ourfelves, or any thing we have, as our own, but the LORD's. His GOD is our GOD, his Spirit is our Spirit, and with him all become ours, and are freely given to us. And on feeing this, we cannot help furrendering our all to him again, continually afking, LORD, what wilt thou have me to do? How fhall I improve every talent I have, to thy glory? O make me faithful, not that I may merit thy love, but becaufe thou haft loved me freely, that I alfo, may fhew my love to thee: and that thou art pleafed to fay, that, In this thou art glorified, viz. in that I bear much fruit, &c. And now, if this be the real cafe with you, if you feel, you cannot reft willingly, till you enjoy the full fruition of GOD every moment; if you are willing, that CHRIST fhould do what he will with you, and fhall take away every right eye from you, if you are made willing to deny yourfelf, and to take up your crofs, daily bearing his reproach, &c. then, though you may be mourning, and in the dark, and comfortlefs, for a time, yet indeed, our dear LORD will

come,

come, and vifit you, and will not leave you in diftrefs but will make his abode with you forever. And
he will water you every moment; for, never did a
kind mother, love her own child with fuch care, and
tendernefs, as CHRIST loves his poor, weak Lambs:
the weaker they are, the more they are entitled to
his care, and tendernefs. The more they can cry,
LORD, thou knoweft that I am the weakeft, and the
blindeft, the vileft, and the moft miferable of any;
and therefore, O watch over poor me, nor leave me
for a moment; leaft I fet up an Idol in my heart, or
deny thee, or forget thee, or grieve thy Spirit. Take
my all into thy hands, for I cannot keep my felf.
May this be the continual breathing of your foul;
and may you never reft, till you feel the full power
of CHRIST's Blood in your foul. This is the earneft
prayer of him, that long to fee you fhine, and grow
in grace here, and in glory hereafter, at GOD's right
hand. And in order to effect this, he is ready to rejoice, in being ufed by your great Shepherd, as a
poor inftrument in his hand, whilft

H. H.

LETTER XII.
To **— G—.

Dec. 29*th*, 1741.

Dear Sifter,

I Find the days of your mourning, are not yet
ended, you are taught to wait all your appointed
time, till your change cometh. He will come, and

will

will not long tarry; and the lower he humbles us, the higher he will raife us up again. Tho' all your early acquaintance, and fellow travellers fhould forget you; yet, you have one Friend that never will, or can forget you; He is all bowels of tendernefs, and compaffion, and fympathy: every thing in him is wonderful! Fear not, you will at laft win the day, and Satan fhall be bruifed under your feet. CHRIST will reign, till all his enemies are fubdued. He is King in *Sion*; and all his enemies fhall be fcattered. What! though there are Giants in the land, we have a glorious Captain. who dares ftand before him! Stand your ground, and let not go your fhield. The trial of your faith is precious. Hope, againft hope, and give as little room as poffible to reafoning. The fooner you will flee, as poor, blind, hard, dead, and loft, to CHRIST, the fooner you will find reft to your diftreffed foul. In him is all your fruit found; and out of his fulnefs we fhall drink freely, grace for or upon grace.

I find, it is not an eafy matter, to root the principle of the old covenant out of our hearts; and to go to CHRIST, for faith, and repentance; for growth, and fruit, for faithfulnefs and power, to keep thefe graces in exercife. When CHRIST calls us to obey, to believe, to repent, to grow, and to be faithful, and fruitful, we are ready to look into ourfelves; and to refolve to work thefe in our felves : and fo failing, we fall to reafoning, and thence to unbelief. Our

dea

dear LORD, will make us acknowledge his fovereignity, and humble our fouls before him, and fee that we are faved by grace alone. That the LORD may keep you by his power thro' faith, is the prayer of

Yours in him,

H. H.

LETTER XIII.
To M—— D—— G——.

Feb. 16th, 1742.

Dear Sir,

I Perceive, when the vail of darknefs is but a little taken away from our eyes, we behold fuch glory, and perfection, fhining in the face of JESUS CHRIST, that we cannot help loathing ourfelves with *Job,* under a fenfe of his favour, that we are brought to be fo nearly related to him. *Heb.* ii. 11, to 15. And then we cry, I have heard of thee, by the hearing of the ear, but now mine eyes fee thee; and therefore, I abhor myfelf, and repent as in duft and afhes. *Job* xlii. Who am I, to be thus honored? What! a child of the Devil to be made a child of GOD! What! my heart, that was a den of thieves, and full of all uncleanefs, to be made a temple of the HOLY GHOST! What! Is the Eternal GOD, my maker, become my Hufband, and Friend! What felf-loathing, and love, and zeal, will arife from fuch difcoveries? What wifdom does the enlightened foul fee in the fcheme of our falvation? How precious is CHRIST to fuch a one? How does he behold him full of grace

and

and truth ? the Pearl of great price, willingly leaves all, and suffers all for him, and counts all things, but *dung and drofs, that he may win him. Phil.* iii. 7, 8, 9. Then all the things of time, that the blind world admires, and follows after, appear in their own true light, toys and vanities, not worth his notice : and while he is by the mere letter-learned, defpifed, and pitied, and looked upon as an Enthufiaft, and a fool; he, with heart-breaking pity, fees them in reality deceived. Soon they will find themfelves blinded, by the GOD of this world , and running headlong, to deftruction : and too many, refting content, as it were, with the candle, of letter-light in their heads, while others know CHRIST hiftorically, and talk of him, as their SAVIOUR. The true believer knows him experimentally. he feels the power of his precious Blood, on his own foul , and can fay, he is altogether lovely and that in him dwelleth all the fulnefs of the Godhead bodily. He fays, that here are true riches, that this is indeed the Pearl of great price, and confequently digs deep for it, and reckons his time loft, but when it is directly, or indirectly, fpent in viewing, and fetting forth the glory of this gift of GOD, to a perifhing world.

How fweet, doth he feel it, to fpeak of him, or fpeak to him ; and to do, or fuffer for him ! None can know the fweetnefs, and reality, of this reft, that is in CHRIST, but fuch as feel fin, to be a heavy burden, and labour hard to be freed from it. And when we

are

are wounded, O how tender, safe, and glorious
a Phyſician do we find him to be ? When we ſee, all
our light darkneſs, then, his light begins to ſhine within us. He, that overcometh the pride, the unbelief,
and unwillingneſs of his nature, and is made willing
to become a fool for his ſake, going unto him, under a
feeling ſenſe of his own miſery, ſeeing himſelf the chief
of ſinners, deſerving to be damned Such a one
ſhall find ſuch ſweetneſs in his love, that he ſhall
never have an abiding reliſh, or deſire for creature-
delights, or creature-approbation, &c. He dies to
himſelf, and to the world, its honors, and praiſes;
and out of his belly flows a well of water, ſpringing
up to eternal life. He now, lives a life, hid with
CHRIST in GOD. A life hidden from the world;
and now has bread to eat, which the world knows
nothing of, and eats of the bread that comes down
from above. *John* vi. 51. &c. And being now riſen
with CHRIST, he ſets his affections on things
above, and hath treaſures in heaven; often feeling
himſelf a ſtranger, and a pilgrim here, waiting for the
happy word, that calls him home. deſireing to live
henceforth, to any other end, but to enjoy, and glorify
his GOD, feeling, the Son has made him free, from
the fear of Hell, or of falling finally, away. He ſerves
his GOD, out of love, for thus ſaving him; and when
he feels himſelf weak, through the fleſh, that is ſtill in
him (though it is crucified, and has loſt much power)
yet he rejoices, in the ſtrength that is laid up in
CHRIST; and counts it an honor, to be enabled to

S   ſuffer

suffer anything, for the sake of the name of JESUS. He longs for more acquaintance, and clearer fellow-ship with him, who is his all. Who died, that he might have life. Whom, by faith, he sees, a full propi-tiation, for him; preparing a mansion for him above. *John* xiv. 2, 3. 1 *John* ii. 1, 2 Self is drawn, or cast down, in him, and CHRIST is set up, so that now, he ceases from seeking his own interest, or praise; seeking only, or chiefly, his LORD and Master's; who having sent his Spirit into his heart, doth make him cry, *Abba Father !* To teach him that, which is hid from the wife, and learned , and which the world by natural wisdom, cannot know. 1 *Cor*. i. 21. This Spirit, applies the Blood of CHRIST, to his con-science , and shews GOD reconciled to him . and that melts him down, to love, and godly sorrow, that ever he should pierce, the lovely JESUS; and makes him cry, LORD, What shall I do for thy great name, while I live, to shew my love to thee ? Now, the soul, feeling its relationship, to JESUS CHRIST, goes to him; and humbly, by faith, lays claim to all his merits, and all he has brought to sinners, by his active, and passive obedience, as his own. For, as the wife, by her marriage, is entitled to her hus-band's estate, so each believer being united to CHRIST, by a lively faith; earth, yea, all in heaven is ours. 1 *Cor*. iii. 22, 23. If through weakness he falls, though his heart breaks, because he offended his dear LORD, who freely forgives him all ; yet he cannot live in doubt, because the Blood of JESUS

CHRIST

CHRIST delivereth, or cleanfeth him from all fin. I *John* i. 7. He now feels, what before he only read, and had a notion of, and can fay, *My Beloved is mine, and I am his.* And fo every new difcovery, of CHRIST's love, transforms his fpirit, and nature, more and more to his image. Then he begins to feel, what is a broken heart, and a contrite fpirit: and then, he feels it more eafy, to forgive injuries, to love enemies, to bear reproaches, to be defpifed, and contradicted. So, being ufed to the crofs, he is more and more perfected, by fufferings, till after having fuffered with CHRSIT, a little while, he is tranflated, to be glorified with him; to exchange reproach, for glory, darknefs, for perfect light: feeing weakly, as through a glafs, for the full fruition, having obtained the complete victory. He wears the crown, among thofe, that came out of great tribulation; having wafhed their robes, in the Blood of the Lamb: and there wait, for the accomplifhing the number of the elect, when he fhall make one, among the heavenly Choir, when CHRIST will come to be glorified in his faints.

    I am, Dear Sir,
      moft humbly, and affectionately yours,
          in our dear LORD.
            H. H.

          LETTER

LETTER XIV.

Feb. 11th, 1742.

Dear Sister,

SURE, you find CHRIST more and more sweet, kind, faithful, and tender daily. I hope you feel, that he heals you according to your faith, and that he is more than conqueror, over all your enemies. Though you seem weak, and unfaithful, you can yet oppose your powerful enemies ; and triumph over them, through your head, CHRIST JESUS ; crying, " Ye tyrants, sin and Satan, CHRIST hath vanquished you both." You shall soon tread on the Adder, and young Lion ; CHRIST will soon come to his temple, and will water you every moment. The days of your mourning shall soon be ended. He being your light, the sun will no longer give you light, by day, nor the moon by night. We can never ask, or expect things too great, from our dear LORD. We never come poor, blind, and naked, to our dear LORD and SAVIOUR, and go empty away , none are sent off so, but the full, the whole, and the easy. Never was a friend so faithful and tender — nor a husband more sympathizing, and watchful. O what valuable love is hid in these words, *My God, is your God, and my Father, is your Father !* And with that love, that the Father loved me, have I loved you ! That was free, infinite, and unconditional, eternal, and unchangeable, everlasting love ! O for faith to lay hold of, and to rely wholly on this JESUS. Amen.

H. H.

LETTER XV.

To Mrs. G——— P———.

Feb. 12*th*, 1742.

Dear Sifter,

BY this time, I hope, you feel, that CHRIST hath vanquifhed your enemies, and, that Satan is more and more bruifed, under your feet. But if you don't feel it, yet, reafon not, you foon fhall find, he is a vanquifh'd enemy. Wait CHRIST's way, and time, to carry on his own work in you, being under his hands, as clay in the hands of the potter. Though you may be now dark, you fhall yet fee light, in his light and though you feem to yourfelf, to be quite bar-ren, and dead, yet life is laid up in CHRIST for you, and fo alfo is your fruit, and fhall be communicated to you, as he fhall think fit. Our veffels, are yet too carnal, to bear much of the fpiritual wine. He muft have his own way, to empty, and humble us, and when we are truly broken, and made meek, and lowly in heart; we fhall find reft to our fouls. And as we believe, we fhall enter more, and more into his reft. Therefore, let us look earneftly into the mat-ter, leaft we fall fhort, through unbelief—— Be not difcouraged: if you feem to be more weak, blind, and helplefs; it is only GOD's way of emptying us, to make more room for himfelf in our fouls, and that he may be all in all. That we may no longer build on any thing in ourfelves, or other creatures, but only on him, the Rock of all ages. He is the *Alpha,*

and

and *Omega:* He begins, carries on, and finishes the work. Whom he once loves, he loves to the end. Those that once, truly eat of his Flesh, and drink his Blood, shall never perish; but are past, from death unto life. And however, tho' they may fall; they shall never fall, finally. O how sure, is that New Covenant, of free Sovereign grace! He has undertaken all for you; and that to bring you home, in spite of all opposition. Where he is, there shall you be soon: He has undertaken to make you meet for glory. He is preparing a place for you — He will be the finisher of the faith, which he himself is the Author of. He is a Shepherd, that will not lose one of his sheep; and such a Physician, as never fails curing; and yet, does all gratis. Go then, with all your sorrows, thro' backsliding, &c. to him; and, he will freely heal you, tho' you have nothing but wounds. *Isa.* 1. 6. v. 7. 17, 18. O come to him, Pray come, filthy, as you are, and he will wash you, and make you clean — and present you, pure, and spotless, before the Father, *&c.*

In Him, I am yours,

H. H.

LETTER XVI.
To his Mother.

Feb. 27th, 1742.

My Dear, Dear Mother,

I Have, sometimes, sweet symptoms, that my work is almost finished — and I feel, that. I am in a straight ftraight which to choofe. Pity, to the dear Lambs, conftrains, on the one fide, and the thoughts of leaving them is fore; but the fervent longing of my foul is to be difolved, and ever be, with my dear LORD. But, between the two, my cry is, LORD, do thy will, let it be what it may —— I hope, Dear Mother, you feel CHRIST in you, going on, from conquering, to conquer; cafting out the world, and the things of time; working in you that mind and fpirit that is in him; deftroying the works of the devil in you. If in order to fet up his kingdom in your foul, and to caft down the power, and ftrong hold of Satan; do not be ftagger'd—If you feel fometimes fome hidings of his face, fome hardnefs, and deadnefs, fome ftrong on-fets of the enemy, Satan; fome bitter remorfes in your mind, and fome fore wounds in your foul—You muft fuffer with him, e're you can be glorified with him: and if your trials are the lefs from without, expect them much the fharper within. Faith is a grace given us to be tried, and exercifed, and fo is every grace—Our hearts, are ready to be carelefs, and negligent, unlefs exercifed by trials; they are all tokens of GOD's love to us, and when fanctified, to fend us nearer to GOD.

O, Dear Mother, my comfort, as to you, is, that I hope our dear LORD has loved you, with an everlafting love; and that he has begun a work in you that fhall be finifhed in glory; and that you fhall not reft, but ftill be kept labouring, and heavy laden,

till

till you find reft in our dear LORD. There is no true
reft, but in his Blood. May you never grow whole,
when wounded, till CHRIST applies his Blood to
you, by his Spirit. Rather be mourning continually,
than be flightly healed. Pray, beware of falfe comfort, rather wait at CHRIST's feet; and then the
Comforter will foon come. Yield not, though you
feem to be overcome the Day ftar will foon arife
in your foul —— Dear Mother, Eternity, is at the
door! Beware of grieving that blefled Spirit, without whom, you cannot believe, or repent — Be much
in fecret — Wait often on GOD — Yield to the motions of his grace in you. Beware of any thing that
fets you in a hurry of mind. There is fuch lovelinefs, excellency, and fuitablenefs, to our wants,
in the LORD JESUS, that, when we begin to know
him, we cannot, afterward, have a conftant relifh,
for any earthly thing. O how fweet will he be, to
us then! When he is efteemed the Pearl of great
price, the only object of our love, defire, and delight;
we fhall then, find him a Rock, that will keep us
from finking, in all ftorms, and trials, a Friend that
will never leave us nor forfake us, a Brother that
loves, with an unchangeable, and everlafting love!
a Hufband that will fympathize with us, in all our
fpiritual afflictions! a Shepherd, that will carry us in
his bofom, while we are weak Lambs! a Phyfician,
that will take care to heal all our wounds, freely, and
tenderly. A Father, feeding us with the milk of his
love, through his word, and that alfo beyond the

love

love, of the moſt kind mother, to her ſuckling child !
although, for our ſins he may, like a kind father, viſit
our tranſgreſſions with a rod ; yet his loving-kindneſs
will he not utterly take away. Pſal. lxxxix. And,
though he tells us, we muſt expect little beſides
tribulation, in the world , yet, he aſſures us of
laſting peace in him. Make ſure then, of him ; let
every thing elſe go, that you may lay hold of him :
count all things but dung, that you may win him ;
and that you may know him crucified, and formed
in you ; ſealing you to the day of redemption. And
when you have known his love, light, and *Spirit*,
under a ſenſe of your ever deſerving eternal flames ;
pleade the privilege of being juſtified freely, by his
grace ; *Rom.* iii. 22, 23. and then you ſhall have reſt
to your ſoul. Which is the earneſt prayer of

Your moſt Dutiful Son,

in the beſt Bonds,

H. H.

L E T T E R XVII.
To Mrs. G——— N———.

Feb. 28*th.* 1742.

Dear Siſter,

YOurs I received, wherein I find you are ſtill
in the fire of affliction. Your faith, and patience, it is likely, muſt bear a further trial , but the
brighter will they ſhine at laſt. The New Covenant
of grace ſtill ſtandeth ſure, and CHRIST is always
the ſame gracious Mediator of it. *Heb.* viii. 6.

T   x, 16.

x. 16. xii. 24. And in him, blessed be GOD, is the same unchangeableness : there, the weak have an equal title to GOD's love, with the strong : He is still a tender, sympathizing Husband, and Friend, and loves us no less, in darkness, and deadness, than when we enjoy light. When no inherent comeliness appears in us ; believe that he is made unto us, Righteousness, and Sanctification too. 1 *Cor.* i. 30. Though, as a Father, he chastises our sins with a rod, yet, his loving-kindness will he not withdraw from us, and his Covenant will he not break, but will turn even our backslidings, and temptations, and falls, at last to his own praise, and our eternal good. O amazing grace ! Flesh, and blood, can neither reveal, nor receive this aright. But what are we, that to us, it should be given, to know what is hid from the wise, and learned ? He deals with his willing people, as if there were no rigorous justice in him, or no law to demand or threaten them. Happy they, who are truly taught to flee from the law, and take CHRIST as their Husband. What have we to do in darkness, but go at his general call, to the unconditional promises ; pleading our misery, and our common interest in him, as the chief of sinners : waiting still at his feet, nor letting go, by any means, what he hath wrought in us : but pleading it, and wrestling with him, without taking any denial. And sure he will come, when it is most to his glory, and least for ours ; and when the trial has answered the end it was sent for. I have sometimes freedom, and love, and power to wreftle, and plead for you; the dear JESUS fets you on my heart: till then I never think of you . I truft, this is a token for good. You fhall not be always mourning, and crying how long? The days of your mourning fhall be foon ended. I truft the time of finging of birds will come. I believe we are too remifs, and cold, in pleading the promiffes, and our intereft in CHRIST, with our dear LORD. It is good to wait, knock, and feek, when we cannot feel; it is good to look up, when we can fcarce fee: for he views the motion of the foul towards him, and will fhew us his pierced fide, make our ftony hearts break; and then we fhall mourn, as one for his firft born. *Zec.* xii. 10.

Yours, in our Dear LORD JESUS,

H. H.

LETTER XVIII.

To Mrs. E———.

Radnor, March 26th, 1742.

Dear Sifter,

HOW fweet, and ravifhing, are the thoughts of death and eternity to the foul that hath heard the Shepherd's voice! To be forever without any interruption from Satan, by trials within, or without, where we fhall be all light, and no darknefs; all love, and no felf; all grace, and no fin. My dear fellow foldier, we fight under a kind, and watchful, and never failing Captain: his ftrength fails not, when ours doth: he watcheth over us, even when we

T 2

forget

forget him, and ourselves : He hath taken the whole work into his own hands — He is our Righteousness, in which we stand equally justified, at all times, before the eye of justice ; and his active obedience is ours, so that though we fall short of the glory of GOD in our obedience, yet his perfect obedience being made our sanctification, wherein GOD looks on us, his holiness can look on us therein, and love, and accept us, even when we perceive millions of imperfections in all we do, think, and say, &c. And thus, through CHRIST, becomes our all in all. We are before GOD, not what we are in ourselves, but what as in CHRIST, and so we become dead to the law, the moment we flee to CHRIST, and the law dead to us, so that as it cannot give us life, by keeping it, so it cannot threaten us with death, or any punishment in justice for breaking it, for CHRIST has, in our stead, answered all its demands — This is foolishness to the carnal world, and hiden from the wise and learned, but, it is the wisdom of GOD in the hearts of such as are made willing to become babes, and fools, and despised, for JESUS's sake. who having found rest from all the fears of the Law, in the Blood, life, and death of our dear IMMANU-EL, we have the Law written in our hearts, and we long for an entire conformity to it, because it is the image of our dear Father. We love holiness, because our Father is holy, and hate all sin, not because it damns, but because it is Satan's image, and contrary to GOD's nature — And the more holy we are, the

the more fruit we fhall bear to our dear Lord. And the more ufeful we will be in his Houfe and Church; the more fellowfhip we fhall have with him, and the more affured ftill we fhall be, to be with him for ever; and the more concern we will bear for his caufe, and intereft, fo much the more we fhall be rewarded. O what foul ravifhing thoughts are thefe, to fee Christ all in all, and felf nothing — to fee God's eternal love, and to fee the bleeding fide of the dying Jesus; and to fee eternal life flowing to us freely from that Fountain. This will make us thirft for that moment when this mortal fhall put on immortality ——— I hope the cry of your foul is, What haft thou, O eternal JEHOVAH, loved me thus! What me, vile me! what fhall I do for thee! when you feem weak, look out of yourfelf immediately unto him, who is your ftrength. Whenever you fall into fin, and fee all you think and do to be fin, then do not reafon with unbelief, but look immediately to him that has no fin, who is become yours by grace, elfe you will give the enemy an advantage over you; but as foon as ye flee to him, then your peace fhall be eftablifhed, and your foul fwallowed up in a deeper admiration of his free fovereign grace, who called you, and made you to differ, when there was no difference between you and thofe that are in the road to hell.

SINCE our dear Lord empowers you to be a Stewardefs over a little portion of this earth, and he reckons what is done to one of his little ones, as

done

done to himself; and as he hath given you a heart to dispose of them, according to his own will; and since his work and cause calls for such helps variously; beware, for Satan will watch to confound you; to make you the less able to do the most good, he would feign be your Counsellor, at least, how, and where to give. You have need to pray much, not only for light to see that what you do, is with a single eye, and out of a true principle of love to JESUS; but also that he may be your wisdom, directing you where to give much, and where but little, and how to lay them out, not only for GOD, but also to bring most glory to GOD: may the LORD guide you. I was stirred up to give you these general hints, to prevent, as far as I could, your love being abused, through the vigilance of a cunning enemy. Good, of various kinds is going on; and calling for the help of every member in his place. Some house-keepers, are poor, and fail to get work, and are near being in want: and, I believe that some who are called to go about, fail to go, as much as they would, by reason of the narrowness of their circumstances — Some things ought to be printed — Schools are much wanted — Many talents, I believe, lay unimproved, for want of help — Many, I view, as called to the Ministry, fail to have necessary education. Society-rooms should be built, and rented — Thus, in general, please to take a hint, that you may earnestly beg of GOD to direct you, how to give your mite, according to his will — This is the desire of your poor, and unworthy Brother, in CHRIST,

H. H.

LETTER XIX.

To M——— D——— G———, Esq;

April 5th, 1743.

Dear Sir,

BE not surprised, if our dear LORD is shewing you, more and more of your helplessness, and inability to believe, and repent, and love, or even to act those graces, that he has wrought in you already. Though they now seem dead, they will be made to blossom, and bear fruit again. We are a very long time, learning to deny ourselves; and are daily prone to backslide from him, who is our Helper, to seek for liberty: and we hear, that true freedom is not to be had in ourselves. Perhaps you are come, by this time, to see more and more of your ignorance in spiritual things; yea that you are quite blind, and can see nothing. This is also the LORD's doings, and it should be marvellous in our eyes; for it is in his light we see our darkness. Our Idol of self-wisdom must come down, as well as that of self-sufficiency. The world, by their own wisdom know not GOD; and, from the great love we bear, to our own wisdom, we are not willing, to become fools, that we may be made truly wise to salvation. Therefore, the things of GOD, are hid, from the wise, and learned, according to the flesh, and the world, but are revealed, to babes, and those who are ignorant, in their own eyes, and the esteem of the world. Whence had this Adam learning, was the old objection,

tion; but GOD, works wifely, through the foolifhnefs of preaching, 1 *Cor.* 1. 19, 21. viii. 27. and ftill
brings to nought, and confounds the council of the
wife. Thus, CHRIST becomes *foolifhnefs to the
Greeks,* that would know him by mere learning, and
the dint of reafon. and a ftumbling block to the
Jews, that would not own fuch a King, who made
no better figure, than to ride on an afs. and had no
better companions than poor fifhermen, yet, he appears truly glorious, and altogether lovely, in the
eyes of thofe, that are taught by him, and are made
willing to become fools, that they may have the teachings of his Spirit. When called to endure croffes,
trials and temptations, think it not ftrange; for our
faith muft be purified. And till we perceive the
depths of iniquity, in our hearts, and the abominable
evil of our nature, we fhall never admire the free,
fovereign electing love of GOD: that called us, out
of many thoufands, and made us to differ, when there
was no difference. We are all prone to fet up our
own righteoufnefs; and thus lofe fight of that righteoufnefs of CHRIST, in which alone GOD looks upon
us with approbation. We fecretly, build on the fand,
of fome work or other, of our own, and fo claim a
part with the SAVIOUR, in the work of our falvation. Thus we, in the pride of our hearts, would
have it, that we make ourfelves to differ, and that
GOD did not love us, becaufe it was his good
pleafure fo to do, but becaufe, he forefaw fome
difference, or that we would make ourfelves to differ;
by improving the grace that he would give us.

　　　　　　　　　　　　　　　　　　　This

This is the language, of all our carnal, proud hearts, while unwilling that GOD, in CHRIST, should have all the glory, of our Salvation. Until GOD shews us, the abyfs, of unconceivable abominations, that is in our vile nature, and that we are in every thing contrary to GOD's pure nature; and how much we deny, and difhonor all his perfections, and alfo break every jot of his holy Law; and thus prove, we are of the very fame nature with the devil, and damned fpirits. And are fully anfwerable to the titles that the Holy Spirit gives us in his facred word, viz, of dogs, fwine, goats, tygers, lions, wolves, children of the devil, enemies to GOD, dead, blind, and rebellious; full of wounds, and putrifying fores. We hear, that the ant, or the wild afs's colt, is wifer than ourfelves; and that none, can caft out the ftrong man armed, the god of this world, that works in our hearts, but he that is ftronger, or Almighty. Then, being thus experimentally, brought to know our own hearts; we cannot be fhaken by the wind of falfe-doctrine, and carnal reafoning; but feeing the ignorance, of the moft wife reafonings that are in the hearts of fuch, who, not knowing themfelves, fpeak to poor fouls, they know not what. Indeed, we fhould pity what we are not able to mend, and endeavour to prevail with GOD, by praying for them; when we fee, we cannot win them, by fpiritual, and experimental reafoning. When GOD, by difcovering our fall, original pollution, and loathfomenefs, brings us to admire that love, and wifdom, that would find out a recovery,

U   for

for such miserable creatures. Then will our enemy
rage, when he sees us, dreading the rock of self-
righteousness, being now convinced, that if we shall
not have the Righteousness of CHRIST, we must
perish for ever. Then, will he stir up, another corruption, in our hearts, *viz* unbelief, or carnal reason-
ing, crying, How can GOD love such a loathsome
creature, and such an abominable rebel, as thou art?
Till GOD breaks that strong hold, also, by shewing
us, that his grace is free, and doth not call the righteous, but sinners to repentance. And when the enemy
fails again, to keep us, by a sight of our vileness, from
going to CHRIST, and laying hold of him, he will
try, to beat us off, from our confidence, and will
strive to tempt us to lay down our shield, by shewing
us our unfaithfulness, since we believed, and also that
we are imperfect, in all our best obedience, saying,
with our modern divinity, that we are justified, by
the imputation of CHRIST's meritorious death, but
that imputation is only conditional, on the consider-
ation of our own faithfulness, and obedience, so that,
CHRIST brought us into a state of salvation, but we
must keep ourselves in it. By these stratagems of
the devil, our poor souls, are long kept in bondage,
till the light of the glorious Gospel, arises more clearly on our souls, and dispels the clouds of errors, where
the prince of darkness dwells. and then, we shall,
by the teachings of the Holy Spirit, see that CHRIST
is made unto us, Sanctification, as well as Righteousness; and that GOD looks on us as holy, and just

in CHRIST; and that his active, as well as his paffive obedience, is imputed to us, and we are thereby, quite freed from the Law, as a covenant. And we fee the whole we need, in him, and that as he began the work, fo he has undertaken to finifh it. And as GOD, by his free love, brought us into the ftate of falvation, He alfo hath decreed, by his faithfulnefs, to keep us in it; and to fupply us, with all graces neceffary, to our glorifying him here, and to all eternity. Dear Sir,

I am yours, fincerely,

in our Dear LORD,

H. H.

LETTER XX.

To the Rev. H—— D——.

April 2, 1744.

My Dear, Dear Brother,

GReat is the honor that is conferred upon us, to be the LORD's Trumpets, and Ram's-horns! But the greateft honor, and happinefs is, in having hearts enflamed with his love, and our fpirits drawn out with pity, to mankind, and to be delivered from the power of felf love, the world's *Diana.* For till we are fo far delivered, from our own wills, and wifdom, as to give place to GOD's, and from felf-love, as to give place to other's intereft, and the common good, in our hearts, and to prefer it, before our own; we are not capable, of any office, in the kingdom of our LORD. For we fhall be afcribing his glory, and

caufe,

caufe, to our own wills; and betraying our truft, to feek ourfelves. This I wrote in the fimplicity of my foul, as the workings of my heart, juft now. I find a little of that pure, and difinterefted love, to fouls in general, now in my heart, and fuch longing to fee fin, root and branch, deftroyed, and to fee GOD, and man brought together, through the wounds, and death of JESUS; that I cannot withold my pen, from communicating, to one who knows what it is, to be enflamed with thefe facred coals. Go on, thou dear embaffador of JESUS, and may thy tongue be always, the pen of a ready writer. Fight, and con-quer — As I underftood, by the laft few moment's converfation, I had with you, your mind is fix'd, and confcience perfuaded, that it is the will of him, that changes not, that you fhould marry dear Sifter C———. Though, I cannot fay, I have had any par-ticular light, in the affair, fo as to affure me, yet I have nothing againft it from GOD. But, as it is an affair, of fuch moment, and as your character is fo public, I doubt not, but from a jealoufy of your own heart, and fear of running before GOD; and leaft you fhould miftake affections, for revelations, you have had many anxious hours, on this account. I would, indeed fympathize with you; for, I fee more, and more, that our happinefs, does not confift, in having this, or that creature, but, in being delivered, from our own wills, permitting GOD to rule, and reign. As one Bro-ther obferved, every creature is to us, what GOD makes it: If we expect any thing, from the graces,

or

or gifts, or feeming fitnefs, of any creature, we fhall be difappointed—The married ftate, is a great myftery; and fuch, as are brought together, by the LORD, fhall experimentally know it. They fhall find in that relation, what is the mutual love, that fubfifts between CHRIST and his Church. This, I am perfuaded, my Brother, begins to learn. I find it is a great thing, to be a hufband, father, and head of a family · to behave in each place as a man of GOD, and an inhabitant of the New *Jerufalem*. O Sir, let us help each other, in our prayers, that as in other things, we go in, and out, before the LORD's heritage. So, in every ftep we take, in this great affair, we may fet a pattern, for the young ones to walk by, or to copy after; who are more influenced by example, than by precept. Let it appear to all, that we feek not ourfelves, but the LORD JESUS, and his intereft. This lay clofe on my heart for a long time, for fear I fhould take any ftep, that may be ufed by our common enemy, to the ftumbling of any—Love of beauty, and the world, is what by our profeffion, of being CHRIST's difciples, we declare againft, and even, after GOD often fhewed me his will, as I thought, on this affair, fear leaft the world fhould think I was led thereby, ftuck very near me. But, after, I had freedom, on this affair, as I thought, from the luft of the eye, and the luft of the flefh, and, even, from trufting in gifts, or graces; when the queftion was put to me, on reading *Jer.* xlv. 5. whether I married

for

for GOD, or myself, I found a myftery of fpiritual felf-feeking in my foul and faw, that ftill I was an Idolater, till I came to marry for GOD, and his Church, and not for myself, but, *only in the Lord.* 1 Cor. vii. 39. And bleffed be GOD, I feel fomewhat of it in my foul, notwithftanding all the evils of my heart; and fince I obtained this, I have found true refignation, and was willing GOD fhould have his own time, and way, to bring about his own will, which, before, I could not find, on clofe examination. I am now going to a *Wiltfhire*-Affociation, and, as I cannot come to *Parle*, for a long time, defire dear Sifter *C—*, to come to *Chapel-evan*, that we may pray, and confer, &c. together.

I am Hers, and Yours,

H. H.

LETTER XXI.

To a young Man that was called to the Miniftry.

Old Paffage, April 6th, 1744.

My Dear Brother,

YOUR cafe lay on my heart; and I had more than common freedom, to cry, that the LORD would fend, teach, lead, and fill you, with zeal for his glory. That he would cover your head, and keep your heart, and tongue, under his own government, to the very end. The liberty, I had, in my own foul, from the Holy Spirit, to lay your cafe before GOD, and plead for you, feems to me, to be a hint, from the

Holy

Holy one of *Ifrael*, that he intends you, for fome fervice, in his Church. He alone, has a right to fend
whom he will, and to qualify each, as he pleafes, for
the work. But, if fo, 'tis no wonder, if you are
bowed down, with a fenfe of your evil nature, and
begin to feel the buffettings of Satan. 'Tis by a
train of experience alone, we can come to know
GOD, the SAVIOUR, and man, in his miferable ftate,
as fet forth, in the Holy Scriptures, fo as to be able
to open divine truths, with authority, and demon-
ftration : and feal them, if called to it, with our
blood. Acquaintance with GOD, and our own hearts,
efpecially, with the glory of our LORD JESUS
CHRIST, is effentially neceffary, to qualify us, to be
his Embaffadors. For, if the love of CHRIST doth not
conftrain us, the difcouragements, that we fhall meet
with, from within, and without, will foon ftop us.
For, when we truly ‾, the nature of the work,
and begin to feel the weight of it, we will, with the
Apoftle, cry, *Who is fufficient for thefe things ?* But,
let not this difcourage my young Brother, but, rather
ftir you up, to look to him, who hath the government on his own fhoulders, and humbly offer yourfelf to his fervice, and under a fenfe of the honor, and
glory of the office, be willing to undergo all hardfhips, to qualify you, for fuch a place. I don't
doubt, but with ftrong cries, you continually, and
earneftly, look up to the throne of grace. foon the
LAMB that ftands on Mount *Sion*, will make himfelf,
and his will, more, and more clear, to you, as you

can bear it. The thirſt in your heart to be uſeful to precious ſouls, comes from him, and though as yet, your knowledge of his will, is but dark, be not diſcouraged, ſince you have begun to ſpeak, let none but him, ſhut your mouth having ſet your hand to the plow, you know, your order is, not to look back; and in the work, the LORD, will make his will more, and more known to your mind.

To day, the war was proclaimed, at *Briſtol*, againſt *France*, and Preſs-warrants are in Conſtables hands, to preſs men, for the land-ſervice, and Marrines. Theſe things call loudly on us, to join in prayer, and humiliation. I truſt, that next general faſt-day (if others will not) we ſhall be enabled, to humble ourſelves indeed, both for our own, and other's ſins; hoping the judgment over us may be averted, and the door be ſtill kept open for the everlaſting Goſpel.

I believe, we ſhall not yet, be given up to Popiſh darkneſs. Pray much, my dear man. O be much in ſecret with GOD; and he will teach you glorious things. Pray, that you may be kept very humble, at the feet of the LORD. Some of the brighteſt angels, and greateſt men, have been ruined, by this ſecret enemy, pride; the danger of it is the greater, becauſe it is ſo hard to know it But, JESUS is above this, and all other enemies. In him, let us reſt; and to his arms I (with all earneſtneſs) commit my dear fellow ſoldier. And am

Yours, for ever,

H. H.

LETTER XXII.

To the Right Hon. the Countess of Huntingdon.

May 25th, 1744.

Honored Madam,

I Took the liberty, fometime ago, to fend a line, to your Ladyfhip, and am perfuaded, you will not be offended, at my doing myfelf, this honor, again. I think, I am conftrained, by the love of that JESUS, who is dear to you, yea, dearer than millions of lives, or titles. His glory, I know, he condefcends, to manifeft in your foul, in a farther degree than I am, yet purified, and emptied enough to receive. However, with my foul in the duft, I muft beg leave, to join, my praifes, to yours, for what he has done, in, and for me, ever fince I faw your Ladyfhip laft. O what an honor it is, to be employed by him, though in the meaneft office, and place, in his Church. Surely then, a fenfe of the great glory, and honor, he has confered on you, moft noble Lady, makes you willing to wafh his feet, and loath yourfelf, with *Job*, before him indeed. O, that all the world, did but behold his glory! and worfhip before him — May he ftill animate your Seraphic foul, with zeal, and divine wifdom, as he has done hitherto, that you may be the happy mean, of bringing the favour of his knowledge, to Court, among our great ones. I think, I feel freedom from him, with humility, to write, in hope your Ladyfhip, fhall be thus honored. I know, he has armed your fpirit,

X

with

that courage, and love, that is invincible; by any feeming impregnable oppofition. When our Lord works, who can let, oppofe, roar, or look terrible? The enemy may, and will (and if the eye looks from God, we may, for a while) difcourage, and weaken our hearts, but, all fhall turn, to the furtherance of the work, at laft.

Dear Lady, A fenfe of the honor (that, I truft, your Ladyfhip is not offended, at my ufing this liberty) breaks my heart, before our dear Saviour. O that I may have a place, in your addreffes to him. Blefled be his name, he favours me now, with a farther fhare, of his fufferings. Indeed, the crofs, which was bitter to him, becaufe the wrath that was due to us, was upon him, he makes fweet to me. Satan feems to have his chain, a little lengthened; the Magiftrates, by the liberty, and order, given them to imprefs idle, and loofe men, for his Majefty's fervice, whom the Country, was burthened with, have fhewn us alfo, how much of the fpirit of *Boner*, and *Jefferys*, doth influence them. They have taken up one *James Ingram*, whofe heart the Lord had engaged to affift me, in my place, and work, to write and copy for me, go on eriands, and take care of my outward things, &c. He had been with me, near an year and a half, and was, when apprehended, at work, at my dwelling-houfe, at *Trevecka*. He hath been confin'd, in *Brecon*-Prifon, about a fortnight, though I fent the Commiffioners word, that I

had

had hired him; and agreed he fhould live, as myfelf. But becaufe it was not for a fpace of time, they faid, "He was no Servant, but under the character of of perfons called for by the Act." They feek for me alfo, and have charged the Conftables to take me: though, they know me to have a fettled abode, at *Trevecka*, and that I have a Mother, and Maid, befides this young man, as a family, under my care. They have, alfo, taken another of our Brethren, a Taylor, to fend him to the army—If the LORD calls, I efteem it the fame, to go home, by a *French* Mufket, or a Sword, as to die a natural death. But, if he does not call, in vain, are all effects, to deftroy us. But, though *Paul* had a witnefs, from heaven, that not one of the men, with him, fhould perifh, yet, he faid, that " If the Sailors, did not abide in the fhip, they could not be faved;" knowing the end, and means muft not be divided. For, as it is a fin, to truft in means, and turn our eye, and dependance from GOD; I think, it is a fin, fo to truft in him, as to flight, or neglect, or not to ufe in faith, all lawful means. Thus we find, our SAVIOUR, and his Apoftles did, and commended. But how to act, in fuch cafes, or what means to ufe, I cannot tell, if I fhould be favoured with fome pioper direction, I truft, it would be ufed to GOD's glory. I fear, I have tired your Ladyfhip, but I am loath to give over, my foul is inflamed in writing, and, O LAMB of GOD, grant that her's, may be fo in reading, and

then

then will be anfwered, the prayers, ends, and real abiding defires, of, Honored, and happy Lady,

Your Ladyfhip's, moft dutiful, and obedient

Humble Servant, in our Dear LORD,

H. H.

LETTER XXIII.

To the Rev. Charles Wefley.

Trevecka, July 16th, 1745.

My Dear Honored Brother,

I WILL forget all diftance, and ufe that freedom, I know, you have love enough to bear with; having had long proof of the truth, and over-flowing of the SAVIOUR's toward me, even to my afto-nifhment, at times. What fhall I fay? but that, according to my meafure, you are near my heart. 'Tis matter of joy, and praife, to me to fee thofe, that move in the moft confpicuous places, in the work of GOD, moft favoured with all the fhining qua-lifications. By thefe, they are enabled to convince GOD's enemies, and maugre all the malice of the wicked, to adorn the dear, and glorious Gofpel. Though I find a cry in my foul, to be peculiarly ufe-ful, and that, from a fenfe of GOD's love to me, and of the great honor of being employed, by fo great, and good a LORD. I fee his wifdom, and care, both of his own glory, and of my real good, in that he doth not, as yet, add to my gifts, and ufefulnefs: be-caufe I cannot bear more. O what depths of ini-guity, lies yet lurking in my heart! But, bleffed be

GOD,

GOD, that I am, what I am. I find 'tis given me, to rejoice at the fuccefs of all others, equally with, if not more, than in my own and alfo, to long infatiably, to fee all that love our LORD, in any meafure; fincerely brought to love one another, every moment. I believe that a great, and glorious work, is begun, on the earth. The LORD is indeed gone forth, and though, for fome wife ends, fome little differences, yet remain in expreffions; and perhaps in our conceptions, of fome things: I am perfuaded, it is his will, we fhould bear with each other, in great tendernefs, and that will bring glory to his name, even when we are in the duft. *Col.* iii. 1, 2. 1 *Pet.* i. 22.

I believe, we have all caufe, to be humbled, before him, and fhould loath ourfelves, that we have not been more tender, of each other; and that we have not been more careful, to avoid offences, before the world. However, I believe, the LORD will wipe away our reproach, and bring us together in time. For the prefent, let us forbear, in great love, and fortify each other's hands, as much as we can. Every one, will have his peculiar thoughts, and ways of expreffion. But, all who hold the head and foundation clear, fhould give, and take brotherly freedom: neither be offended, nor put the worft conftruction on others, but, endeavour to underftand fully, the whole of what each mean; but where am I going? You fee, I give my heart, its full vent, I am fure you are not offended, at my freedom. When I find

perfons

perfons of any denomination humbled, at the SA-
VIOUR's feet , and made acquainted with the myftery
of his blood, by his Spirit; I love, and honor fuch.
And though, according to my light, in thefe, may be
many things amifs; yet, when I fee, that the LORD
has revealed his Son in them, and given them a
true, and lafting faith in him, I wait, being affured
all other things fhall be foon added.

BLESSED be GOD, I can fend you good news,
from hence, the Gofpel never ran with more glory
than now, and Satan rages horribly, in his chain,
biting and roaring, as if he would fwallow us up alive.
But, bleffed be our LORD, who tells us, he has but a
fhort time to reign. Laft week, we had a meeting
of Minifters, and Labourers, that help in the work,
and the LORD was indeed among us. The breach
that was like to be made, is I truft, ftopped up effectually. The Brethren, that were for difputing, being now fatisfied—Brother *Rowlands*, was gone to
England; and could not return to us, Brother *Da-
vies*, Brother *Williams*, and Brother *Powell*, &c.
brought glorious news indeed. Congregations every
where increafing, frefh doors opening, and, as it
were, a new commiffion given; many called, and
wounded, whilft others were fo favoured, with views
of our EMMANUEL, as to be kept up whole
nights, finging his praifes, being fo filled with his love,
that they are obliged to cry, " LORD hold thy hand."

The

The Gentlemen in part of *B——ſhire*, and *C——ſhire*, hunt us, like *Partriges*; but ſtill, the work proſpers. There are four preſt, now in *B——goal*—One was a private man, another a *Welſh* School-maſter to Mr. *Griffith Jones*; one was preſſed laſt year, and they then, would not take him; and the other taught an *Engliſh* School, and exhorted, and is full of faith——Theſe are kept exceedingly happy, in their ſouls. With my hearty reſpects to Brother *J——*, in hopes of a line, in anſwer. I remain,

Yours moſt affectionately,

Humbly, and heartily, in our

Dear LORD JESUS,

H. H.

LETTER XXIV.

To the Rev. Griffith Jones.

Briſtol, Jan. 26*th*, 1746.

Dear and Honored Sir,

IT is, with ſincere eſteem, and warmeſt affection, I ſit down to trouble you with this, aſſuring you, that my ſoul is drawn up in thankfulneſs, to our dear SAVIOUR, for the many valuable gifts, and graces he as beſtowed upon you. Particularly, for giving you a ſpirit, to make a ſtand, againſt ignorance, and prophaneneſs: but more eſpecially for ſucceeding your labours with a bleſſing, even beyond expectation; in this our poor benighted Church, over which, my poor ſoul, has often wept bitterly, labouring amidſt

trials,

trials, from all quarters, which none but he that views all secrets, knows, still willing to bear all, and to have my honest attempts mistaken, and ill judged. Still resolved to go on in faith and love, expecting our dear SAVIOUR would give such as it most immediately concerned, a clear right judgment, of this work, wherein, I have been counted worthy, to take a small share, that at length, our *Zion*, might once more, become the praise of the whole earth, and sit as once she did, as princess among the Provinces. How has my heart rejoiced, at any branch, or kind of revival, that seemed to appear in any shape, tho' it may seem, to be darkened by my poor labour. I think, I find this in my inmost soul, let my name, and labour, ever be forgotten, only let our SAVIOUR be known, and adored; this truth searched, received, believed, and preached, and his poor despised Church, raised out of darkness, and formality, to her former faith, and love; and once more put on her beautiful garments. This alone is all my desire, and I am persuaded, of all the hearts, of the other Labourers, that are thrust out to labour in this way. Often have we wished, and prayed, that those who are in power, did but know really, our motives, and aims, and the difficulties we struggle with, for the real good that is indeed done to souls, and still proceeding; sure, their bowels would move within them, and their judgment of us, would change; they would no longer think us mad Enthusiasts ———

WHAT !

WHAT! though in our zeal againſt the prophane, and ignorant, we might mingle ſome of our nature; drop ſome ungaurded expreſſions; and, in ſome things, for want of more experience, go too far, and perhaps be impoſed upon, by ſome deſigning hypocrites, ſhall no other ſide be ever viewed, but that? are there no conſiderations, to ſoften the charges laid againſt the work? Are not we ſorry, for giving juſt offence to any, or for ſhewing a ſpirit, of improper behaviour, contrary to the Goſpel? Do we not openly, before the world, acknowledge, and bewail, all our infirmities? and profeſs our earneſt deſire, after a thorough conformity, to our SAVIOUR's example and precepts? Though we are refuſed regular admiſſion to the Communion, and doubtleſs, for reaſons, that ſeemed to our ſuperiors, ſufficient; according to the light in which we are ſet before them. And though we are publickly, from the pulpit, reproached, and branded, with that which do not belong to us, and tho' many of us have, in our own Pariſh Church, been refuſed the Sacrament; for no other reaſon, but frequenting our Societies. Yet, we do ſtill determine to continue in prayer, for our deſolate Church, and to abide in her, until, totally put out. I know too well, her ſpiritual poverty · though ſhe in her fallen ſtate, is ready to ſay, ſhe wants nothing. The work done among us, is too evident, to be denied, and too manifeſt to be concealed, or need any proof, that it is, as to the bulk, and ſubſtance of it, a work of the LORD tho' clouded with ſome unavoidable weakneſſes, which charity, on time, and

Y

folid

folid confiderations, will cover. Yea, we have ven-
tured our lives, for feveral years, under all manner
of difcouragements, in the face of an angry world;
frequently in danger, of being ftoned to death,
fometimes appearing with our blood mingled with
the duft, without any provocation, but becaufe we
invited them to the SAVIOUR of finners. Whilft, the
LORD knoweth, we had no other motive, conftraining us, to travel inceffantly, day and night, through
exceffive rain, wind, hail, froft and fnow, difcourfing on all weathers, in the open air, but love, to GOD,
and his Church; promifing ourfelves, and wanting
no other return, in this world, befides what we had,
in our own confcience. Enduring fcandals, hard
fpeeches, and reproaches; efteeming this reward
enough, to find poor ignorant prophane wretches,
crying out, " What fhall we do to be faved ?" Breaking off their fins, in righteoufnefs, following the
LORD, they once blafphemed, and bringing forth the
good fruit of obedience, in their future lives. This
reward, we undeniably have, though feveral tares
grow with the wheat, that make a fine fhew, and
then turn out bad, and bring an evil report, which
we have feen with breaking hearts. Yet, bleffed be
GOD, there are feveral thoufands in *England* and
Wales, that prove by Gofpel characters, they are
enlifted into the army of Chriftians indeed: to
whom the LORD has made us, means of falvation,
plucking them, as fire-brands, out of the burning.
O did our fuperiors know, only the hundredth part,
of the real good done, I am perfuaded, they would be

fo

fo far from difcouraging, or thinking ill of the work, which fo evidently befpeaks its great Author, that they would enquire more into it, till they fhould be fully fatisfied, on juft evidences ; fo that whatever mixtures, of Enthufiaftic flights, hot zeal, or other irregularities, might join with it, in urging the truth , yet, I am humbly perfuaded, many of the mafters of our *Ifrael,* would with tears, or praifes, fall down before him that fits upon the throne, and fay, " Verily, the LORD has vifited our land ; and this is the LORD's doing. Who befides, could open the eyes of the blind, and turn the wicked, from the evil of his ways, and make the profane fcoffer, an humble, perfevering worfh.per of GOD ? Inftances are, through GOD's help, innumerable. I am fure, as you fee, and feel, the ftrength, weight and burden, of the great work of dealing with fouls, and are not infenfible, of the trials and fnares that furround us, from the various kinds of people, we have to deal with, from the invifible enemy ; and above all, from the unfathomable depth of iniquity, that was born with us. You can not help weeping over us, before the LORD , and that it is a miracle that our heads are kept above water. O dear Sir, Who is fufficient for thefe things ? If I had not a well grounded perfuafion, that the work is the LORD's, and that he hath undertaken to bear the care, weight, and management ; my hands would hang down, under a thoufand confiderations. And it is by this humble dependance, on the grace, wifdom, power, and faithfulnefs, I fee in him,

that

that I move. O Sir, help us in your prayers, for never was such weak, unworthy, insufficient worms, employed in so great a work. How will it at last bring him honor, and praise, before men and angels, for ever employing, and blessing in any degree, such poor, and justly despised instruments. Your cautions, about pride, &c. are always seasonable, and blessed to me; for I can never sufficiently, prize the privilege, of faithful exhortations, I need them continually. When I am made in some measure, poor in spirit, I soon forget my nothingness, and need of fresh supplies of grace every moment, or that I stand by faith alone. What would become of me, if our dear, and faithful Redeemer, did not provide thorns for my flesh daily; a fresh buffeting continually? How happy it is for me, that of a truth indeed, by his own order, I believe, and hold fast, that he has undertaken to die for me; and that because he lives, I shall live also. being kept, by his power alone, through faith to salvation. O help Sir, help in the great, yea, very great work of endeavouring to snatch many poor sinners, as brands from the fire; pray help us, for the LORD's sake, all you can every way. *Zec.* iii. 2. *Judi* 23.

Yours, for ever, in the best Bonds:

H. H.

LETTER

LETTER XXV.

To J——— I———.

Plymouth, Feb. 8th, 1746.

My dear Brother,

JUST now I came to Town, and read your kind Letter, and could not help setting pen to paper, immediately; not doubting, but by this time, the devil is overcome, and my dear Brother is now brought to live by faith, leaning on the Beloved, JESUS. Rejoicing by faith, because the LORD liveth, and reigneth forever. By faith, seeing wheel running within wheel, to carry on the eternal plan. By faith, crying, LORD, thy will be done, all is well. By faith, committing soul, body and all to JESUS, the SAVIOUR. By faith, seeing the government of all, on his shoulders. By faith, triumphing over sin and death; even when both seem strongest, and most lively. By faith, living when we are dead, and conquering, through the great victory, obtained on Mount *Calvary,* even when we feel ourselves, seemingly led captives. By faith, seeing one that is invisible. By faith, living, fighting, walking and rejoicing, on that strength, and grace that dwelleth in CHRIST JESUS our dear SAVIOUR. Thus, by faith, let us walk in the dark, as in the clearest light, and sing in heaviness, and give glory to GOD, taking him at his own word. And then we shall be able, to preach this life of faith, to others; and so lead the Lambs by faith, out of the reach of Satan. I sympathize,

pathize, indeed, with my dear faithful Brother, in his conflicts; yet by faith, I rejoice, in the honor that my dear Brother is going to receive, after his humiliation. In this faith let not my dear Brother be afraid, of any oppositions. Thus,

I remain, yours, affectionately,

in our dear LORD,

H. H.

LETTER XXVI.

To Mr. J—— B——.

London Feb. 18th, 1746.

My Dear Brother,

EXpectations of seeing you, deferred my answering your kind Letter sooner. We must be united, and love one another, very dearly, for, I feel your life is my life, your food is my food, and your GOD is my GOD. May we ever lie in the dust, and we shall be mutual blessings to each other. Without controversy, great is the mystery of godliness indeed. O thou mysterious EMMANUEL! reveal thyself to thy poor witnesses, and let thy glory fill the whole land. Amen.

SINCE I came here now, the LORD has been very kind to us, he is returning apace, to the despised *Tabernacle*. All disputing hath quite ceased, and we go on harmoniously together, and I believe, the LORD has taken the work, quite into his own hands. Then say you, I am sure, it will go on, and prosper,

and

and ſtand. We are now ſettling the Society in claſſes, and reſettling all the ſcattered Bands. I have been through every Claſs, and the LORD has been, and will be with us forever. What are we, my dear Brother, to be thus favoured? Many propoſe to join the Bands, and Society—We had a letter from Mrs. *Whitefield*, giving an account of the progreſs, of the Goſpel, in *America* The *Indians*, and *Negroes*, are baptized, twelve or fourteen, in a day, and many of them are filled with the grace of the Holy Spirit! O glorious Goſpel-days! Let us all unite our forces, and go forth, through the aſſiſt-ance of the LORD, the Eternal Spirit, againſt the mighty. Thus ſoon we ſhall ſee greater things than theſe. I ſaw Brother *S*—, laſt Sunday, and he ſays the LORD bleſſes the Brethren, beyond the ſea. Let us therefore unite, in one ſpirit, at the throne of grace, for the general ſucceſs, of the everlaſting Goſpel, of our dear LORD and SAVIOUR, in whom,

I am Yours,

H. H.

LETTER XXVII.
To Mr. —— H——.

London, *Feb.* 18th, 1746.

My Dear, Dear Brother,

GLouceſter is much on my heart. I muſt write a line to you, becauſe I love you indeed, and ſhould rejoice, to be made the inſtrument of refreſh-ing you. I am not unmindful of your trials, but he

that

that bought you, with his own Blood, and counted you worthy, to speak for him, will take care of you; and keep your redeemed soul, near himself, that you may reign with him here, over all temptations, which surround you. Satan will not fail, to attempt, making you ashamed of the cross, but, I am persuaded, I shall find dear, yea very dear Brother *H*———, enabled still to adhere to *Moses's* choice; and to look at that glorious crown of immortality, that is set before us. Go on, my Brother; and trample by faith, on all the golden baits, and allurements. and hold fast your integrity, and you shall be honored indeed; and become a pillar in the temple of GOD. Hold fast that, whereunto you have attained, and let no one take your crown. Great indeed is the honor of being employed by the LORD of Hosts, in carrying messages to his precious children. Though now they make but a poor figure in the eyes of the poor blind world; yet, I am persuaded, they are precious, and the only truly great, and noble, in your eyes.

LAST week, I had a Letter from dear Mrs. *Whitefield*, dated *Sept.* 29*th*. I saw another from Mr. *Whitefield*, of the same date, the LORD continues to be with him, blessing his labours more, and more. He has had the offer of 500 *l. per Annum*, at *Pensylvania*, but the LORD enabled him to trample upon the golden bait. When our enemy can not discourage us, by opposition, he will strive to tie our hands by flatteries, and allurements: but faith breaks

through

through all. By this time, he has been at *Georgia.* Matters go on harmoniously here, now ; Brother *Edwards,* (the Prince's man) hath joined us , and we are happy together. The fcattered flocks begin to be gathered, and reunited. We are now fettling the Society, and refettling the Bands. Frefh doors are opening , we want more labourers. Let us all unite, in the fpirit of the LORD. I am perfuaded, your foul cries, Amen.

I am, with moft cordial refpect, to your felf, and Spoufe, and fervent prayers for the little one,

Yours, for ever, in the beft Bonds,

H. H.

LETTER XXVIII.

To Mr. T—— J——.

London, Feb. 22*d,* 1746.

Dear Brother,

HOW is it with, and among you ? I was in hope of a line, but I truft, our SAVIOUR is leading you by the hand, and fhewing you more of the glory, and myftery of his Perfon, fo as to transform you into his likenefs. Are you in any trials inwardly, or outwardly ? Fear not, all is well JESUS reigns, and lives for ever: and you are bone of his bone, and flefh of his flefh. Let your faith ftill feed on his Flefh, and drink his Blood, till you feel you are one with him. Go on then, highly favoured of the LORD ; let not thy hands hang down, or thy heart fail , the LORD of Hofts is thy everlaft-

ing

ing ſtrength—Rejoice, and make thy boaſt in him, all the day long. Remember me to dear *S——*, let her alſo, be ſtrong in the LORD, and in the power of his might. Soon, ſower, and reaper, ſhall ſit down together, at the marriage ſupper of the LAMB, and rejoice for ever — Let this ſuffice for the preſent.

THE LORD is with me, in public, and private work, and bleſſeth Brother *I——* alſo. This is enough, to have CHRIST our SAVIOUR in all! O, the myſtery! that this Man is GOD! He wept, travelled, bore cold, pain, hunger, and thirſt; all reproach, ſhame, and all other miſeries for me— My loving everlaſting Brother, Sure this LORD, is love! My ſoul within me is loſt, in wonder—and melts like wax—O this love, this myſterious, unfathomable love! May we never ſpeak of it, without a deep ſenſe, of the profound myſtery, on our ſouls. Amen. May the dear SAVIOUR, and his great love, be ever before your eyes: then you will be willing, to endure all things for his ſake,

In HIM, I am Yours, for ever,

H. H.

LETTER XXIX.
To Madam B——.

London, Feb. 22d, 1746.

Dear Madam,

YOU will not be ſurprized, that I ſteal a moment, to aſk you how it is with your ſoul? If by faith you are enabled to keep from all wanderings, ſimple, fimple, and child-like, at our SAVIOUR's feet, I am perfuaded, that all is well, your faith above, humility and meeknefs, praife and refignation, mutually take place, to beautify and adorn your happy foul. But if it is an hour of temptation, and needfull, the fiery trial muft continue fome time longer, then in patience poffefs your foul, being affured that all, even the darkeft fcenes, fhall concur to bring about the great end God's glory is your prefent, and eternal happinefs; if fo, then all is well. The foreft humblings are before our exaltations, if ftorms do but go before glorious palms, then, welcome all. let us rejoice in the midft of all, becaufe the LORD reigns, and is our all, and rules, difputes, and orders all in his Church, for the good of his people. Then it is fweet, fafe, and happy, to be in his hands; and it is our priviledge, and reafonable fervice, to be as clay, in his hands, giving ourfelves wholly to be difpofed of as he pleafes, equally thankful when he frowns, and when he fmiles, this is his will, and our true happinefs. I am confident, that he unvails more, and more of his glory in your foul, and fheweth you more of that myftery, the word made Flefh —— This is indeed food for our fouls, and fhall be our entertainment for ever: in this eternal light,

I remain Yours, in CHRIST,

H. H.

P. S. My kind refpects, to all the Family.

LETTER

LETTER XXX.

To Miſs. G———.

London, Jan. 3d, 1747.

Dear Miſs. Sally,

MAny trials, I am perſuaded, you meet with, from within, and without, as I know, you are determined not to reſt, till CHRIST is revealed to you. The SAVIOUR makes me heartily ſympathize with, and take this liberty of ſhewing my gratitude to aſſure you, that all difficulties, muſt, and ſhall ſubſide. Faint not, nor be weary in your mind, but, bear the trying hour ; if the LORD ſee, that you muſt be in heavineſs for a moment, by manifold temptations, it is but for the furtherance of your joy, in the end. After you have ſuffered a while, and been deſpiſed, and caſt out of the eſteem of many, you ſhall come out of the fiery trial, as gold tried, and a veſſel of honor fit for uſe. Let nothing move or diſcourage you, but go on ſteadily, meekly, and boldly ; the Prize ſet before you, is worth leaving all, will, and affection for ; the SAVIOUR you follow is one you need not be aſhamed of ; and faith can ſee a glory and excellency, in his true, faithful (though mean and deſpiſed) followers. By faith, *Moſes*'s choice was ſoon fixed — as I am perſuaded, dear Miſs. S——— is, and that you are ſo far from being ſhaken by any winds that blow, that you only take the deeper root, and ſtrive the more to bring all around you to be inwardly, and feelingly acquainted with that Man who died

between

between two thieves, who is the eternal GOD—
the only true happiness, and the one thing that
all stand in need of. O remember 'twas he first loved
you, and not you him ! let him then have all the
glory ; and while you walk humbly before him, he
will go on to reveal his goodness to your soul, and so
you shall grow more like him, and more happy in
him. For his sake, I am, dear Miss S——, with
sincere respects, to as many as you think proper in
the family.

Theirs and Yours, most cordially
in our one common LORD
and SAVIOUR for ever,
H. H.

LETTER XXXI.
To Mr. G——.

London, Jan. 3d. 1746.

Dear Sir,

I Trust our SAVIOUR, our dearest LORD, and
GOD, does continue to draw your heart from
the spirit of the world, to his dear self. O, it is our
happiness to be raised out of the vices, and principles, and hopes, and fears of this world, so as to see,
that it can neither make us miserable, nor happy.
Dear JESUS, O thy condescension ! thou Incarnate
GOD ! How can I behold him in a Manger, who fills
all the heavens, with his glory ! My GOD, my SA-
VIOUR ! Why are we not continually ravished with
thy love ! Here is room, for a noble mind to employ

its

its deepeft thoughts, in reviewing the height, and depth of this unfathomable myftery! here let our hearts be found, whilft the worldly mind is bufied, and perplexed about its toys and fooleries. Dear Sir, This is happinefs indeed, to be inwardly acquainted with him, that bled, and died on the tree. I doubt not but your prayers for, and indefatigable labours with your family are made fuccefsful; and if difficulties fhould arife, be not difcouraged; all hearts are in the hands of him whom you ferve the Eternal Spirit can foon wound, and foon heal, caft down the moft lofty imaginations, and foon reveal the great Atonement for the remiffion of our fins. Has not God given you an earneft for good already? Let faith and patience have their perfect work. They that feel the Saviour's love will not be offended——Dear Sir, I greatly long, once more to fee, and tell you what grand things the great God is doing on the earth. O what mercy it is, that we fhould be born in thefe days of Gofpel light! Therefore let us be all on the ftretch for God, whilft thefe golden opportunities are in our hands. I am, deareft Sir,

more heartily than ever,

Yours, moft humbly, and Affectionately,

in our dear Lord Jesus,

H. H.

LETTER

LETTER XXXII.

To Mr. T—— J——.

London, *Jan.* 4th, 1747,

My Dear, Dear Tomy,

I Am forely fatigued ; it is near three in the Morning, but, I muft tell my dear Brother, how dearly I love him, and his.   How is it with you all ? Doth the vail wear off ? and doth the glory of a crucified SAVIOUR appear brighter and brighter.   O my Brother, that Man is indeed the Eternal GOD : what views, doth he give vile me, of himfelf at times ! He fhines brightly, like the noon-day fun. As yet we know nothing to what fhall be revealed.   O what heart of ftone would not melt, to fee the eternal GOD, lying in the Manger ! Sweating, and tired ! wearing his thorny crown ! not opening his mouth, becaufe he bore our fin and fhame ! O my dear Brother, Where fhall I begin, or end ? What fhall I fay, but fall, and bow, and wonder ! Go on my dear Brother and be bold in the great myftery of GOD, become a Man.

In him, I remain Yours, moft affectionately

and heartily for ever,

H. H.

LETTER XXXIII.
To the Rev. D. Rowlands.

London, Jan. 4th, 1747.

My Dear, Dear Brother,

I Truft, this fhall find you, viewing that great myftery, God made Man ; here we muft come, this is the end of all knowledge, and the root of our happinefs ! O my Brother, here let us be for ever, loft in wonder and amaze ! Now in writing, my foul melts within me —and I feel, I long to leave this body of fin, behind me, to view this transforming fight. Will you call me *Moravian* or *Antinomian* — God forbid; it is the life of my foul, and no borrowed plume, nor heated fancy, but my folid happinefs. O that great Atonement ! When fhall we be all loft in its infinite depths ! Are there any that abufe this Profound knowledge ? it is becaufe they have not the thing itfelf, but the fhadow. O that I had faith to abide in this light continually; then would I no longer be a fervant to any fin or Idol, but would fhine in the image of God. O pray for me, that I may have more faith, that I may know more of this wonder of all wonders, Christ crucified——But whither am I going, fhall I be tempted that I offend my Brother by this language ? No, no, I know thee better, my deareft Brother : methinks I rather fee tears of adoration, trickling down your face —crying, " This is the one thing needful, I alfo want to know indeed, that by this faith, I may really become dead to fin, and alive to God in all things."

HERE

HERE are many gracious, growing, lively souls, and several are added lately.

I am, My Dearest Brother, and Fellow-Labourer, with heartiest respects to Brother *Wms.* and all the Brethren, and Societies; longing to see you all.

Yours in the best Bonds for ever,

H. H.

LETTER XXXIV.

Jan. 15th. 1747.

My Dear Friend,

I Certainly thought it long, to have no opportunity of sending you a line, all this time, but I have often carried you on my heart to the Friend of sinners. When I see the infinite care for us, GOD as the eternal Spirit has taken us for his peculiar charge, I can rejoice over the little scattered, weak, foolish, simple children, yea triumph in their behalf, over all the designs of an inveterate enemy. When I see them engraven on the heart of the great High Priest, and markt out by him, and his infinite bowels yearn over them, I then break out into singing, and cry, " Fear not little flock, whatever lions, wolves, or tygers come against you, they shall not devour you, because the Shepherd never slumber nor sleep " Go on then dear Brother, be not discouraged at any seeming obstacle; for as sure as faith is given, it shall be tried; but rejoice in tribulation, because the LORD is GOD. Remember, thou art passed from death to

A a

life—Thou art come to Mount *Sion*, and to the Blood of fprinkling—O then let every thing help to drive thee to thy own Strong-hold, the Clefts of the Smitten-Rock, and there bathe thy foul continually in the running ftreams of a SAVIOUR's infinite Blood. Remember, every thorn we have in our flefh, every fall from GOD to felf, proceeds from our flighting that fountain, and our wandering from it, and growing felf-fufficient, and lofing the lively fenfe of our vilenefs and nothingnefs—O let every thing help to bring us down to the duft, at our SAVIOUR's feet, to make us nothing before the LORD; that he may be truly honored in us, and by us, in all his perfections, as one wholly entitled to our whole hearts, and to be the fole object of our truft and confidence, of our love, delight, and moft pure obedience. Think what infinite condefcenfion it is in him to look at all, on fuch vile abominable worms as we are! O let us all give him the glory, for he is worthy. Stand amazed ye heavens, and be aftonifhed O earth! What! is the great I AM become a Man? and, is his delight, with the children of men, and with the vileft of them too? It is in this character alone, I muft addrefs him, and lay hold of his free love, and believe he is my GOD, and Father——O LAMB of GOD! Art thou my Hufband, and Friend for ever? And didft thou, O Infinite Purity, fee me, in all my filthinefs, and then come by me, and fay to me, Live, live! And didft thou then clearly fee, what a myftery of wickednefs was nefted up in my abominable deceit-

ful

ful heart? and didſt thou then ſee what I ſhould be, and yet not only adopt me into thy family, but give me the honor of waiting on thy Bride, bearing thy name to the Heathen, and for thy own honor s ſake, rather than turning me out of my honor and office, wouldeſt cover all my faults? O Lord, then ſhall not I be willing to waſh the feet of all, and to be for ever the ſervant of all, and be always thy paſſive clay —— Is not this the language of thy ſoul, my dear Brother, as it is the language of mine? Remember, he that humbleth himſelf ſhall be exalted, ſaith the Lord — I truſt, thou doſt live in the experience of that great privilege, purchaſed for us, and entailed upon the whole family, to be granted us, on making a proper, humble, confident demand of it, viz. a deliverance from the power of that tyrant ſelf-love, and pleaſure, of our own wills. To be ſhut up in the chains of this monſter, is the miſery of all miſeries; but O the happineſs of this liberty, to be able to ſay, at all times, not my will but thine be done, this we have experienced, let us then maintain our ground, I ſhall rejoice to hear of thy proſperity, alſo how our Saviour's work in thy ſoul, and how the little Society goes on? Remember me moſt tenderly to them, and may we all be on our Watch-tower, for all eyes are upon us, and above all, the eyes of our eternal Father, and Redeemer Jesus Christ. Lord be merciful to us, poor ſinners —— I long to ſee you all, but am going from hence, to Briſtol —— In the mean time, let us meet at the Throne of Grace.

I am Yours in the beſt Bonds,

A a 2

H. H.

LETTER XXXV.

To Mr. Kinfman, at Plymouth.

London, March 19th, 1747.

I Long to hear how you go on, trufting that our dear SAVIOUR doth become more amiable in your eyes, drawing you from every thing to himfelf, doth caufe you to weep and mourn before him with godly forrow for all finners, and the want of conformity to him in yourfelves, and others——O when fhall he reign as King, in the hearts of all his followers? When fhall every thought, and motion within us, be brought into fubjection to him? Sure, this muft be all our cry, as we grow more acquainted with him; we fhould then long to have the fame mind which is in him, and defire to love, as he loveth, and to behave to others, even towards the rebellious, as he hath to us (even when we were nothing but enmity) with forbearance, patience, and love — Pray let us always contend for all the fruits of the Spirit, and especially faith, love, and humility, that by our fruits, all may be obliged to own, we are his difciples. My cry is, and has been, that my lot may be caft, among fuch as indeed, are without guile, and funk deeper and deeper in true poverty of Spirit, into the loving Spirit of JESUS, and to love his redeemed ones, in him, as poor finners, in themfelves, notwithftanding all infirmities, that may appear to me, in them, either in judgment, or practice.

My

My dear Brother, if our SAVIOUR intends you for any further fervice, in his great and glorious family, let your heart be prepared for trials, of all kinds: from within and without, from the world and the Church, from the prejudices, weakneſſes, and corruptions of the Lambs, of the flock, and from the finifter views, worldly wifdom, and pharifaical tempers, of carnal profeſſors, much more from the bigotry, and narrow heartednefs of others, that fhall come among us, to difturb us, and that according to their light, for confcience fake. But let not my dear Brother's heart fail him, under thefe and a thou-fand other confiderations, though every difficulties, that fhall indeed meet you. But, let it make you cry mightily, for the witnefs of the Holy Spirit, to fee your work and place; then you will be able, in fa th, to charge the LORD with all your burthens; and to expect all ftrength, wifdom, and inward, as well as outward qualifications, from him who em-ployed you: Then you will not run away from the work, nor be worfhiped by man or devil, or your own heart in it, but thankfully embrace the crofs, feeing it the higheft honor, and privilege to fuffer trials, as well as to be active for the LAMB's bride——O my Brother, a great work is begun on earth, and where it will end, GOD only knows, but happy thofe that fhall be employed in it.

TELL the Society, I remember them, and longing to fee you all again — with my love to your fpoufe,

I am Yours, moft heartily, in our dear LORD,

H. H.

LETTER XXXVI.
To Mr. Edwards.

May 10th, 1747.

My Dearest Brother,

LAST night I came home, read your dear Letter, and soon felt your burthens. I assure you, my dear Brother, that your burthens are mine— Be not surprized, or moved, at any thing you see within or without—they all come to you through the Bloody Fountain, and have but one voice, and that is love, and peace———We are now in the furnace, but we shall soon come out. Blessed is the man that endures temptation, and abides with our SAVIOUR, in the hour of trial. Be stedfast, and immoveable, let faith and patience be your armour, you are sure of victory. I wish you could stop your eyes, and ears to all that grieves you, and only look to the wounded SAVIOUR. But if Brother *Adams* and you, had more freedom together, it would rejoice me, for I know your hearts and eyes move the same way; and it is Satan only weakens your hearts, to each other, surmising jealousies by bad tongues— Let nothing weigh down your righteous soul a moment, I am sure we shall do well. I trust you will find in me an open ear and heart, with sweetest sympathy, to bear your burdens, for if I am trained up, for any usefulness, it is for this. If seeing all the evil that I ever saw, read, or heard of on others, in my

own

own nature—will eafe me of a felf-righteous, defpifing fpirit, then I muft in fhort, come down. And I can have full freedom with none, but fuch as fee themfelves chief of all finners, like beafts, and more like devils. If daily trials, from fome fpirits or other, will inure me to forbearance, and break my fpirit, fo as to make me fympathize with fuch as are afflicted, fure I muft , for I know of no other happinefs, but to be bruifed, and trodden under foot, and defpifed, for Jesu's fake   Greater blifs and honor, cannot be conferred upon us, nor am I never happier, than when, by contempt poured on me by fome, judging, and cenfuring of me by others, and by the fight of my felfifh, devlifh nature, I am brought to the duft under the feet of all men, willing to be reckoned as the off-fcouring of all things.   Then I ftand amazed, and bow, and wonder, and adore an incarnate God ! And feeing my felf, and Brother *Edwards*, and all our wicked Brethren complete in him, fing, and rejoice in the midft of all, and moft heartily fubfcribe myfelf, my dear *John*, your wicked, forrowful, rejoicing, unhappy, happy Brother, and fellow fufferer, in Christ our Redeemer.

H. H.

LETTER

LETTER XXXVII.
To Mr. Gambold.

London *July* 2d, 1748.

My Deareſt Brother,

I Was refreſhed by the receipt of your kind Letter, and am thankful to the great Prophet of the Church, that leads you on in divine light, and eſpecially with every freſh diſcovery, keeps your ſpirit humble before him; it is the meek and lowly, that he will continue to reveal himſelf to, and honor and erect in his kingdom. Every diſcovery given us by the Holy Spirit, is worth millions of worlds — May you abide ever as clay in the hands of the great Potter; and you will ſee greater things than theſe. O my Brother, we know nothing yet as we ought to know: we are but babes; but we ſhall pry, by faith, into this Infinite wonder, till we are ſwallowed up in light, in viewing the incomprehenſible Majeſty, an Infinite FATHER, Infinite SON, Infinite HOLY SPIRIT —— Myſterious Incomprehenſible THREE-ONE! Infinite Majeſty in our own nature — This ſhall be our ſtudy, and view, and contemplation, and bliſs to all eternity —— It is now a time of building the temple, no wonder then, if it is a time of confuſion, and much duſt ariſing, and if there is much noiſe, &c. only let the labourers love one another, and mind their own work. Every member has its proper office, Bleſſed are the peace-makers, ſays the LORD — We have more and more reaſon to think

our

our SAVIOUR, has thoughts of love, to this Nation, and Church; he is carrying on his work, several ways, and takes great steps. Let us bow, and wonder! Fall down, adore, and cry, thy kingdom come.

Now, in him, with heartiest affection, to all his friends, about you. I remain, my dearest, Fellow-heir, of all the promises, and Fellow-citizen of the *New Jerusalem.*

Yours, in our loving IMMANUEL,
to all Eternity,
H. H.

LETTER XXXVIII.
To Mr. J——— Beaumont.
London, *July 2d,* 1748.

My dearest Brother,

I Have been for a fortnight, in the Counties of *Kent,* and *Essex,* or I should have answered yours sooner. I was in hope of seeing you here, by this time; however, if our infinite Master has ordered you to speak of his glory, elsewhere, I am satisfied. I love to see his Bride, in her beautiful garments, causing all around her, to gaze at her beauty, speak of her fame, and be obliged to own, she is indeed the LAMB's Bride, and his Epistle, legible to all. O my Brother, I know of nothing in the LAMB, that shines so strong on me now, as his bowels of compassion, pity, and tenderness, whereby he forgives me, bears with me, hides, and covers all my infinite provocations; who hath revealed this his mind

to

to me, and his patience, in bearing with all my ſtu-
pidity, dulneſs, and infinite ingratitude : unfaithfulneſs
towards others, and my want of ſoftneſs, and moder-
ation, towards thoſe who are far behind, and yet in
the dark. O my dear Brother, we are brought to an
infinite eternity, of love, light and glory, let us ſhew
to all, that we live on love, pity, and compaſſion,
by ſhewing it daily, more abundantly, to all, weak
and ſtrong, bond and free let us appear like our
Father, eſpecially in mercy, and forbearance, in which
he delights We are clothed with love, we feed on
love, we drink daily the fountain of love, we ſee
nothing but love, before, behind, within, and without, in time, and to all eternity ; let this appear, in all
our ſteps O how am I aſhamed, that ſo little of the
condeſcenſion, and kindneſs, and bowels, of this love
appears, in all my conduct ; eſpecially, towards the
weak Lambs, of the precious flock.

You know, and remember, our Aſſociation is on
the 20th Inſtant. As the 14th is like to be a day
very diſmal to nature (the Sun ecllpſed) we thought
it may be of uſe, to meet that day at 10 o clock, to
humble ourſelves, before our Saviour, for all our
ingratitude, and unfaithfulneſs to him alſo for all the
contempt put upon him, by all, in general ; profeſſors
and profane, directly, or indirectly ; will not you
join, and be directed there by that time, and ſend
all about, where you can, to all the Societies ?
That with one cry, we might encompaſs his throne,

to

to intreat him, to wash us all in the Fountain? That he would enlarge the borders of his own kingdom, by carrying on the work himself, both visibly, and invisibly, but rather, the latter. O may he continue to us, the honor, of being his poor, simple, broken-hearted witnesses; especially pray that this infinite honor might be continued to the vilest rebel, that ever breathed —— I have no time to enlarge, I long to meet you in the realms above, where we shall be all light, and no darkness.   I am Yours, for ever,

in the GOD-MAN,

H. H.

LETTER XXXIX.

To Mr. Baddington.

Oct. 20th, 1748.

My Dearest Brother,

I Am glad to find by yours, that you are come to the Fountain; may you there abide for ever. O stand fast in your liberty: many begin in the Spirit, and end in the flesh. Are you so surprised at my silence? did you but take a turn with me, for two or three Months, and see my labours, and trials, &c. and especially could you take a turn, through my heart, your surprise would cease. However, I will inform you, It is now about nine weeks, since I began to go round *South*, and *North-Wales*; and this week I came home from my last journey, round *North-Wales*, I have visited, in that time, thirteen Counties, and travelled, mostly, 150 Miles

every

every week, and difcourfed twice every day, and fometimes, three, or four times a day. And in this laft journey, I have not taken off my clothes, for feven nights, and travelled from one morning, to the next evening, without any reft, above a hundred Miles, difcourfing at midnight, or very early, on the Mountains, being obliged to meet at that time, to avoid perfecution, one man was obliged the week before I went there, to pay 20 *l.* near *Wrexham*, to Sir *W. W—— Wynne* feveral of the hearers 5 *s.* and one 10 *s.* who had paid before · this being the third time the poor people have been ferved thus in that neighbourhood, for affembling together. Laft time, there was only one of our Brethren, went to prayer, with fome of the neighbours, in the family, Sir *W——* triumphed over the poor people, and faid, We have fent for law againft them, but could find none. LORD, anfwer for thy felf, and appear in thy own caufe. I had in another place (near the Town of *Bala*, where I was formerly like to be murdered) a blow on my head, near violent enough, to flit my fkull in two, but I received no hurt. I never faw fuch crowds coming to hear, nor more glory among the people, many hearts, and doors, have been lately opened; we know of feveral who have been awakened lately, and the LORD feems to turn his face towards the rich, feveral of them have been this journey to hear me, and feveral more fpeak with affection of coming to hear Mr. *Whitefield*, when he

comes

comes. Pray remember, me moſt affectionately, to all the Brethren.   I am Yours,

Moſt happy, for ever,

H. H.

LETTER XL.
To Mr. M——

Oct. 21ſt 1748.

My Dear Brother,

THis week I came home, from a very long journey, and found a complaining Letter, from dear Mr. *M.* I ſoon felt his burthen, as my own, and carried it to him that can, and doth bear all our burthens. And by his own eternal Spirit, have you not yet learnt, that whom the LORD loves, he chaſtens, and whom he exalteth, he humbleth, and every veſſel, for any uſe, muſt be again and again purified, and emptied from veſſel, to veſſel? Fear not, after much darkneſs, comes great light, a bondage precedes liberty, as Winter doth the Summer. The deſtruction of our own will, wiſdom, or righteouſneſs ſeems at firſt to come near our very life. However, let us not be dejected, nothing happens to us, but what others have gone through already, who now join the ſongs of triumph, before the throne of GOD. I am the leaſt in the family, and know nothing, but this I have learnt, that our wiſe Phyſician, uſes ſtrange medicines, to reſtore our health, and uſes one corruption, to deſtroy another, of a more dangerous nature; and though we often know it

not,

not, He is ever with us in the fire, and in the water, as well as before we go in, and when we come out. By these trials then, you will be rooted, and grounded in all the truth—you do profess, and have in a measure learnt of GOD, in the furnace, you will learn indeed to admire free grace, to adore a crucified SAVIOUR, and walk humbly before him, feeling true love and pity, to all poor sinners, seeing yourself the chief of them, giving all glory, where it is due. These are lessons never learnt at too dear a rate. I long to see you, and all the little flock, if happily I might be honoured with bringing a message from heaven, to them all, tho' I see no prospect of seeing you soon, my heart and prayers are sincerely with you. I have written to *London* about you, but cannot now settle my round, till the next Association; and as the time of Brother *Whitefield*'s return from *Scotland*, is of some uncertainty, we cannot exactly be fixed about the time of our next meeting. However, this I am sure of, you are all on my heart, so far as I know it. I beg most heartily, to be remembered to all:

And am Yours, for ever,

in the Bleeding LAMB,

H. H.

LETTER XLI.

Jan. 14*th*, 1749.

My Dear Fellow Soldier,

I Received a Letter last week from you, which I snatch the first moment, I have, to answer.

Can

Can I forget my deareſt Brother, who is not only born of the feed royal, but alſo engaged in the ſame war, and ſent out on the ſame errand ? Let earth, hell, ſin, and ſatan combine, thou man of GOD, thou Captain of the living GOD, reach forth thy hand, and in the ſtrength of the moſt High, we will wade through the waters, trample on ſcorpions, triumph in the flames, rejoice, and leap over every wall, enter, and poſſeſs, the good land of Promiſe. Go on, thou Herald of the LORD of hoſts, ſtir up thy ſelf, the LORD, the LORD GOD Omnipotent, the glorious, Almighty JESUS, reigns over all worlds, even the world of ſin and corruption; He rules, yea, over-rules, and terminates the great Ocean, gives it command, and lo, it obeys him ! I freely put my ſhoulders, under my dear Brother's burdens, according to the ſmall meaſure of grace given, and rejoice in his preſent hour, becauſe it is a ſure token, of your farther uſefulneſs, and freſh approaching glory, *Halelujah*. *Eph.* vi. 10, to 14.   1 *Tim.* vi. 11, 12.

To Arms, to arms, my Brother ! cry aloud, ſpare not, tread down the foe, like a mighty conqueror ! let him know, thy commiſſion has to it heaven's Broad-ſeal, that thy weapons are not carnal, but mighty thro' GOD , rejoice, and ſing, in the midſt of all; for all is well, all is yours. I am now ſetting out on a round, for above a month, which prevents my writing to our dear Brothers, *Adams, Edwards, Stephens,* and *Meredith,* &c. Read this, if you pleaſe,

to

to them, with my heartieſt, and inmoſt love, in the
boundleſs ocean, of JESU's precious Blood. There
I am, with kindeſt reſpects, to all the Society, and
eſpecially, all the Brethren, that meet in conference;
moſt heartily theirs, and yours eternally, in him that
lay in the Manger,

and now Reigns on High,

H. H.

LETTER XLII.
To the Rev. Mr. Whitefield.

Oct. 15th, 1749.

My Dear Brother,

I Feel your life, peace, health, and remembrance of
you, peculiarly dear to me, becauſe you have
left all, to go about to call poor ſinners, to find ſalvation, by faith, in the dear crucified SAVIOUR. The
preaching of his croſs, in the Spirit, will break down
all before it. O, my dear Brother, The wiſdom
and pride of man, hinders the glory of that Man, who
is the eternal GOD, from ſhining on the church.
Happy, and highly honoured, is the man, that ſhall be
counted worthy, to open his infinite wounds, before
periſhing ſinners ! Go on, and blaze abroad his fame,
till you ſhall take your flight, to bow among the
innumerable company, before his unalterable glory.
O LAMB of GOD, ſhew us thy glory, and manifeſt
thyſelf to us ; ſo as thou doſt not unto the world.
LORD, I am aſhamed, that I ever took thy tremend-
ous name, in my unclean lips, for I am as a brute
beaſt, before thee.

SINCE

Since I came home from *London*, I have had the infinite honor, of being employed by him, in public and private, almoft continually, fo that I could hardly, even now, fpare a moment, to fend you a line. I hope, I left the fouls in *London*, in a good fpirit, and found thefe fo in *Wales*. Things appear ftill with a better afpect, I hope, in time, to fee fouls joined together, like living ftones, by the HOLY GHOST; and each coming to fill his place, then, and not till then, will the work go on; and the whole camp move regularly, happily, and in order. When each efteems his Brother, better than himfelf, and feels the need of every one, yea the leaft Brother, knowing the mutual dependance, of every member on the whole. You heard of the miferable end, of that great oppofer, Sir *W——— W——— W———e*, may this make us, and all our oppofers tremble, with cries, and tears. I believe that great glory is at the door, and woe be to all oppofers, in the church, or in the world; that fhall ftand before him, when he cometh in his dyed, glorious garments, to judge poor finners.

I am, my deareft Brother, under the fprinkling, of his cleanfing Blood, Yours in all refpects, for ever.

H. H.

LETTER XLIII.
To Mrs. Whitefield

Oct. 16th, 1749.

My Dear Sister,

I Hope, that by all means, you are brought to the facred Blood, of the LAMB of GOD , by this alone, we are brought nigh, and make our robes white, and overcome our fpiritual enemies, it is by this alone the ciftern of our hearts, is cleared from the guilt, polution, and power of fin. O infinite Fountain, what would become of us, were it not for this foul-cleanfing, and fin-deftroying fpring! I truft, the LORD JESUS, is daily teaching you, and fubduing all your wifdom and will, to his own, and making way for frefh manifeftations of his glory, in your foul. One view of him, in his eternal Godhead, and fo, of the Infinity of his Perfon, love, obedience, and fufferings, is worth millions of worlds. Who can fet forth the riches of his death, and the unfathomable abyfs, of his fufferings? the inexpreffible evil of fin appears here more clearly than if we faw all the mifery of the damned. Here, had I more faith, fhould fee more of the fall, the glory of the covenant, the riches of grace, the perfection of GOD, the privileges of believers, the nature of the Law, of fin, death, heaven, hell, and judgment meet in the garden of *Gethfemane*, and on *Mount Calvary!* than all the wifdom, and reafoning in the world, could ever difcover. Hither let us repair, my dear Sifter, and reft our fouls here

for

for ever. Here, let us learn all our Chriſtianity. This is the Gate of Heaven, the City of Refuge, the Eternal Ark, the Brazen-Serpent, the one thing needful we want to know. O come my dear Siſter, let me take you by the hand, and ſhew you one, even JESUS, the eternal Word, the LORD JEHOVAH! groaning under the load of our ſins, bearing them away, in his own ſacred body, to eternal oblivion! drinking up the river of eternal wrath lying in the way, encountering with all hell, in reſcuing our ſouls from the jaws of the Lion! O let us adore, though we cannot comprehend, let us bow before the Infinite Sufferer, and pray, that he would be pleaſed, to turn the myſterious Streams, into our parched hearts, that we may become like a watered garden. It is here, in tracing my dear Maſter, and GOD, in all the ſteps of his humiliation, that I feel my pride ſubdued, my will broken, and my carnal wiſdom, nail'd to the croſs, here, I ſee the whole Church, our SAVIOUR's dear Body truly precious in all its parts to me, and ſee every thing dangerous, that comes as a vail, between me and his glory. O my loving, my dear eternal Father, I am aſhamed, that I have ſtill ſo much of a Jewiſh heart, that neither ſees any glory in thee, or in thy death, or feels any of thy Infinite pain, in my ſpirit. Certainly I deſerve millions of hells, for ſlighting thy Wounds, and Blood, for thinking, and ſpeaking of, and feeding ſo little on thee, thou glorious Sufferer! O my dear Siſter, we ſee but little of

the

the evil of defpifing, or forgetting this adorable
Fountain. O the great Atonement, when all the
Types of this, are fo glorious, what muft thou thyfelf
be ? If the fhadows that were to vanifh, were of fo
great account, what muft the fubftance be ? By this,
that infinite evil, fin, is removed, and we the finners
are faved. Eternal torments, pungent plagues, and
curfes are removed, and we, the heirs of hell, become
heirs of heaven ! If we were not ftupid, hard, and
very carnal, this would be the fubject of our thoughts,
and converfation, as well as preaching, continually.
Every mercy we enjoy, fpiritual, temporal, and eternal, all come to us by this Door, and preach a crucified SAVIOUR. Had we but fpiritual eyes, and
ears, to perceive and difcern, the valuablenefs of the
Atonement ! I have been tedious, but I dare not
excufe myfelf. I rather rejoice in the freedom of
fpirit I find, and as it comes from the heart, I am
perfuaded, it will go to the heart.

I am Yours, for ever,

in the fpotlefs LAMB,

H. H,

LETTER XLIV.
To Mr. T—— B——.

Oct. 16*th*, 1749.

Dear Brother,

I Thank you, for yours, and was made glad for
the leaft blefling, attending the word dropping
from my vileft lips to any, it is reward enough

to

to be honored, if it were to fpeak but one word
with a bleffing, in all our worthlefs life. I hope, you
are coming more and more, into the clear light of
God's Holy Spirit, out of nature's darknefs. Then
you will fee God himfelf, clothed with our humanity,
and lying in all the forms of humiliation, to exalt us
to glory, it is our happinefs, to view this, in his
light, then we fhall fee heaven opened in him, and
every fin, with the fiery Law, and all its curfes, with
death and hell, removed out of our way. and we,
that were the heirs of hell, now in him, made heirs of
heaven, in everlafting glory and immortality, kings,
and priefts, unto God. Such news as this, well
underftood by faith, will make Brother T—— cry
Halelujah, again, and again. Christ is worthy, of
all praife in heaven, and on earth, for he hath redeemed us, with his own precious Blood.

In him, I am Yours,

in the beft Bonds,

H. H.

LETTER XLV.
To Mr. Cox,

Oct. 17th, 1749.

I Often think of you with joy, becaufe I fee you
are faved from all things here below; and building your neft, in the cleft of the Rock, growing as
a twig, in the eternal Vine, living in his life, viewing endlefs glory, in his bloody mangled Body,
which many, are fo far from feeing, all together
lovely,

lovely, as white, and ruddy, that they cannot bear to hear much of him, in that defpifed form. But, let us mind the rock from whence we were hewn, and remember, we were a Rib, taken out of his fide, and whatever others think of the matter, he is made of GOD, unto us Wifdom, Righteoufnefs, Sanctification, and Redemption; he is our life, hope, ftrength, and our all in all. Let us adore him, in all the forms of his humiliation, in the Manger, and on the Crofs (when all defpife him) as well as on the throne; and confefs indeed, we are witneffes of this, that his Flefh is meat indeed to us, and his Blood is drink indeed, and in him, we that were loft, are found, and acquitted fairly, from the curfe, and fecond death. Don't you fee yourfelf, fo effectually faved in him, as if you had never finned, nor had ever been a fon of *Adam*, and an heir of hell? Amazing grace! glorious falvation! enough to dazzle the eyes of all the angels! But fo it is, I, the loft, damned rebel, am eternally faved, *Halelujah!* Will you not affectionately remember me to your fpoufe, and Sifter? *&c.* Beg of them to plead their mifery, before our crucified LORD, GOD, IMMANUEL, till he fhews them heaven, and eternal life, opened on Mount *Calvary,* and they have the witnefs of it in their own fouls, by the Holy Spirit——let me now fubfcribe myfelf

Yours, affectionately in the Bowels of

The loving IMMANUEL,

H. H.

LETTER

LETTER XLVI.
To Mr. Gambold.

Dec. 27th, 1750.

My Dear Brother,

I Am now come home, after finifhing a circuit round *North*, and *South Wales*, and have been refrefhed with your favour, of the 23d *ult*. I cannot but highly efteem, the acquaintance of thofe who are favoured with the fpiritual knowledge of that Man, who is the wonder of all worlds ! and our only comfort and friend ! My happinefs is to view him, and all the fullnefs, of the Godhead, in him — and myfelf, one of his dear members. But my fhame is, that I abide fo little in him, and that I live fo little out of my felf in true poverty of fpirit, before him. Yet notwithftanding all this, I can fay, that he is my life, and becaufe he lives, I live, and fhall live alfo. Our poor country-men, make great oppofition, to the preaching of his death — few fpirits can bear to hear, that this Man, is GOD — and that the Immortal, died —— But, in every country, there are fome, that defire to know nothing, but JESUS CHRIST, and him crucified. Great crowds flock to hear the joyful found, notwithftanding the *Jews*, and *Greeks* oppofe themfelves moft vigoroufly, and do all they can, to veil the glorious Sun, but truth is mighty, and ftill prevaileth. How our SAVIOUR intends hereafter to difpofe this branch of his work, we know not, but that he really has a great work carrying on

among

among us, and that he is laying the foundation of a plan, againſt raſh oppoſitions, that in his hand, will ſurmount all difficulties from all quarters, is very evident.

I ſhall eſteem the continuance, of your correſpondance, a particular favour——I am now in great haſte, but ſend hearty ſalutation, to all I know, the Brethren with you, and to your ſpouſe.

I am theirs, and Yours, moſt affectionately,

Now, and for ever,

H. H.

LETTER XLVII.
To the Rev. Griffith Jones.

Trevecka, Jan. 3d, 1760.

Dear Sir,

I Was much refreſhed in hearing by *Thos. David* of your being yet here below, to ſtand in the gap, and to interceed for a poor unbelieving world, which being indeed, blinded by the GOD of this world, ſee no glory, or excellency, in the moſt precious Redeemer, but run really, in the broad way to eternal ruin, and that merrily, and happily ; and I greatly fear, but very few mourn over them. I hope you will live to awaken many, by your honeſt labours before the end of your time. I ſhould eſteem it the higheſt honor, if counted worthy, to be of ſome real ſervice to all, eſpecially to poor *Wales*, as you have been hitherto in many reſpects. From an apprehenſion of our

danger

danger at this time, from the tyranical fpirit of popery. I have accepted a call to go with fome of the honeft people that are here with me, in family, into our Militia, to finifh my labours, and life, if GOD pleafes, in withftanding our enemies, in the field of blood. A life, by far, the moft difagreeable, to my nature. But by the faithful Spirit of grace, being perfuaded of my duty, am willing, to teftify once for all, my regard to my King and Country; but above all, to the moft precious Gofpel: and let him who bled for me, and whofe I am, do with me as feemeth good in his fight. Commending myfelf, and mine, in the moft earneft manner, to your prayers; wifhing you all the bleffings of the new Covenant, the precious fruits of our SAVIOUR's life, fufferings, and death, with eternal healings in, and under the Redeemer's Wings.

In him, I am, dear Sir,

with all due refpects Yours,

H. H.

LETTER XLIX.

To E—— M——, and E—— R——.

Torrington, Jan. 1ft, 1762.

My Dear Brethren, in the Grace and Truth of JESUS CHRIST,

WAS he not GOD, clothed with my nature, full of all the grace I ftand in need of, I could not move on one ftep, but as he has been in the world, and on the crofs, and is now in glory, as our Head, and High-Prieft. I ftand, and fet up my Ebenezer, and love, and highly honor, all that real-

D d

ly

ly venture on him ; and honor him, in this world of unbelief. where self, and carnal noise abounds This may come to you, I hope, as a new Year's gift—Surely my heart is so much with you, that nothing, but the clear call of our Redeemer, could keep me thence, a moment. This day reminds us our SAVIOUR was circumcised for us, went under the Law, entered upon our work, and became a servant, both to circumcise our hearts, and to deliver us from the servitude of the Law, also to make way for streams of purity, and holiness, to flow into our unclean hearts.

O my Brethren, we are happy because our SAVIOUR is above all, and never changeth ; and the more we venture on him by faith, the more he will honor us. Then stand up for him, in the face of all seeming impossibilities ; faith does indeed remove mountains, and overcome all things.   How highly are you honored, in being counted worthy, to bear up our SAVIOUR's name, and truth, and to wait on those souls who are gathered together, by our most dear Redeemer.   Stand steadfastly then, in him, and always say in your hearts, he is able, and he shall reign. He will perfect his strength, in your weakness, and doth use the weak, and foolish things of this world to confound the wise, and strong.   It is he that worketh, therefore do not hinder him, or by unbelief, spiritual sloth, and indolence, but still cry, I am the clay, and thou art the Potter, form me as thou wilt. Still shew, that you love the SAVIOUR, by watching

carefully

carefully, over his Lambs, and be faithful over the little he has entrusted you with, always finking in true poverty of fpirit, at his feet, each efteeming the other better than himfelf. In this faith and fpirit, I am, my dear Brethren, Yours, for ever, in the truth.

H. H.

LETTER L.

Barnftaple, June 19th, 1762.

My Dear Wife,

SHall this find thy Spirit bowing, to the great compaffionate Redeemer? weeping before him, for all thy backflidings from him? It is cerainly both fweet and fafe, when we loath ourfelves, before him, becaufe we are not more like him, and do not abide in him, but fo often triffle with him. Whenever we can fubfcribe that confeffion, *That we are, indeed, the chief of finners,* and the leaft of all in GOD's houfe; whilft we continue thus poor in fpirit, meek, and lowly in heart, our SAVIOUR is then very near us, will be ever bleffing us, and giving us frefh proofs of his love, and affurances of his grace, that he will never leave us, but that we fhall be with him for ever. may you be keept thus wakeful, looking to our LORD JESUS CHRIST, then wilt thou grow in grace, and be always happy, though the mountains be removed, to the bottom of the fea, whatever happens then, you will be meekly refigned,

and

and give thanks, and fay, the LORD is King, and he fhall reign for ever. O remember, he is your all, that he has loved you, and he will never change. that he is able to finifh, as well as to begin his good work ! Remember, that you are his, and your whole bufinefs in the world, is to do his will, to feed on him, love, and live to him. In this faith you have left your father's houfe, to take up your crofs with me, this day eighteen years. And this day twenty-feven years, he firft admitted me into his prefence, by giving me his Spirit, to cry, *Abba Father*, and fealed that truth on my heart, that he doth not change. I have found him to be, certainly, the Unchangeable I AM, to this day. Shall I not have your fpirit, thoroughly with mine, drawn from nature, to grow in the faith and poverty, of our dear Redeemer? then will you be ever thankful, that he has called you out of the world, out of the reafons and affections of perifhing nature, to deny your felf, daily, to take up the crofs, and to follow him, and him alone, by faith in the regeneration, to poffefs all the fruits of the bleffed Spirit, in which, I am, in earneft prayer for thee, that thou mighteft come out of every thing, that perifheth, to live on the Bread of life, for ever.

I remain thine,
most affectionately, in all truth,

H. H.

LETTER

LETTER LI.
To all the Family at Trevecka.

London, Jan. 11*th* 1763.

My Dear Brethren,

BLessed be GOD for ever, for opening a way for us poor worms, out of all sin and self, to himself, by his own Incarnation, and sufferings, which the Holy Spirit hath taken upon himself, to explain, and apply to our blind, unbelieving hearts. An infinite honor he has indeed conferred upon us, by calling us out of the spirit of the world, to live out of our selves, on him, who gave himself a Sacrifice for us. O rejoice in him, and in the work he has given you to do. Pray endure him, when he comes as a Refiner; and with his winnowing fan, to separate between nature and grace, or to purge you from dross, that you may be more fit for his use. I am persuaded, you add to the debt of love I owe you, by continuing to pray for me. I can, to your comfort, assure you, that your joint prayers prevail, for I was never more graciously dealt with, by our SAVIOUR, than in this journey; surely, I can join that old Martyr, Bishop *Hooper*'s confession, " LORD, I am hell, but " thou art heaven." I hope, my journey shall not be in vain, or lost, O that glorious Man ! the only Friend, and delight of his true followers, the fulness, or perfection of the Godhead, dwells in him bodily ! shall we his poor little children not be his care ? Shall we be honored as his house, and be really employed by him,

to

to do fome little fervice, here below? And is it poffible, fhall we be in light, viewing his glory, and bowing before his throne hereafter, for ever? 'Tis certainly fo, for he has loved us, and will not leave his work in us unfinifhed, as he is, we fhall completely be! Let this be our life, joy, and ftrength. O be not weary, in his work and fervice, which you do for him, and not for your felves——It is honor enough for me, to be counted worthy, to be any help and bleffing, to you at all. O praife the dear Redeemer for me, for fure, I owe him, more than all, if I could, I would fummon the whole creation to adore him. O that I was ever viewing him, and feeding on him, and making a grateful facrifice of every thought, word, and moment of time, to and for him! this is furely my cry, and all my ambition, to be found in him, to be his wholly, and that I fhould never grieve his Spirit. O how dear, are you all, there, to me! becaufe he loves, and has collected you to his own houfe; and counted me worthy, to be a father to you! O that I could make you the happieft people in the world, and fet all your hearts in a continual flame of love, to the dear Redeemer, who has bought you, with his moft precious Blood. Thus I am, my dear brethren, and fellow fervants, in our SAVIOUR's kingdom, with my beft love, and prayers for you all,

Your unworthy Father, Friend,

Brother, and Servant, in CHRIST JESUS,

H. H.

LETTER

LETTER LII.

Oct. 6th, 1763.

My Dear Wife,

SHall this find you at the SAVIOUR's feet, pleading his promises and condemning thy self, sensible of thy real blindness, and weakness? when we are poor in spirit, he is ever nigh us, and turns all our evil, to good. O that I could so write, as to set his wounds, and death exceedingly weighty, and precious to thy heart, then is the true end of writing answered. —O thou dear Redeemer, be thou ever amidst our spirits, and reveal thy glory to us, till we shall come up to behold thee, face to face, by thy inesteemable love, and grace. He is, and shall be, my life and sole delight. His will shall be mine, for ever. He is exceeding gracious to me, and feeds me in green Pasture; I cannot doubt, but that he is in the midst of you all, there; for you are his little flock; and he cannot forget his patients, or his few sheep, in the wilderness. O love one another most ardently, and watch over each other, that you fall not a moment from him; for he alone is our heaven and bliss. When we sleep, forget, and turn from him, it is though his great love, and tender care, that he rouses us by any means, till we return truly to him again. O keep with him in prayer, and watchfulness, that thou mayest confess, own, honor him; and then thou wilt comfort the heart of thy husband, preaching the truths of our SAVIOUR's kingdom.

Yours affectionately, for ever,

H. H.

LETTER LIII.

To the Right Hon. the Countess of Huntingdon.

Trevecka, Nov 11th, 1765.

Honored Madam,

LAst week, I received your favour, by which I found, our SAVIOUR honored you, with a little of the feeling of what he went through, when a poor Man, here below. We are too little acquainted with him in all his humiliation, by that revelation of faith, or by drinking of the cup, that makes us feel, what he went through, all his life, from Satan, and from hard, unbroken spirits, that did not know him, but judged only by outward appearance. He leads us gradually to view the mystery of his Person, sufferings, and glory. And it is only in our spirits, that we can know, what he went through, when he cried "My soul is exceeding sorrowful, even " unto death," and this, we must know feelingly, if risen again, to reign with him. Our nature may be brought, by a superficial knowledge, of him, and by common illumination, &c. to do, and be active for him, but to love the cross, to suffer with him, and to follow him, through the streets of *Jerusalem*, from *Gethsemane*, to *Golgotha*, dumb, without opening his mouth, is what we like to see painted in affecting images to work on our passions, but it is what we are too little acquainted with in our spirits. I had a feeling of your trials, and also a spirit to lay them on him, for whom you suffer, who will not only sup-

port

port you in them, but will shew you, they are your crown, make them so easy, that you will esteem them exceeding light; considering what he went through, and what millions, of bright and glorious spirits, now before his throne, went through. And the great weight of glory, he has in store for us, after we have suffered a while; our trials, are gentle Fires · he corrects, to purge out our unseen-self, that we know nothing of. I am, in the best Bonds,

Your Ladyship's most obedient,

Humble Servant,

H. H.

LETTER LIV.

To the Right Hon. the Countess of Huntingdon.

Trevecka, Sept. 26th, 1766.

Honored Madam,

THE fellowship I have with your spirit, in the knowledge, of the humiliation and sufferings, of that dear mysterious Man, our dear LORD and GOD, JESUS CHRIST, draws my pen to paper. Though we may mistake, and lose sight of the real, and honest meaning, of each other's spirits, for a moment, during this very short time of our trial and imperfection, yet that secret feeling of love we have by the Holy Spirit, survives all. Go on and prosper, in all your well meant zeal, to awaken a sleepy nation, to prepare for the glory of GOD's amazing appearance, to judge his rebellious worms. who came in a mean human form, to purge away our sin,

E e

and

and mifery, by the Sacrifice of himfelf. O this wonderful Sacrifice! how blind, and unaffected are we
towards that myfterious Fountain, opened on the
crofs! O the depth of our fall, that we can think, or
hear that God, became a Man, fhed his infinitely,
pure, and Holy Blood, to wafh us in that only puri-
fying Fountain, and not feel every moment an age,
till we behold his face! What is all, within and without, but this? This is the uniting point, the center
of all union—Here, we forget all names, and prejudices, and can truly think of nothing; but love,
adore, wonder, and be happy. I truft, your Ladyfhip is well acquainted with thefe things, by frequent reflections—I can, thro' grace, teftify that
this is my life, for above thirty years; and, all life
but this, is only felf, in fome fhape, or other. All
that live out of themfelves, on this great ATONE-
MENT, are dear to me, and fo, I am perfuaded,
are fuch, to you alfo. To bring all to this point,
is, by grace muft, and ever has been my fole
bufinefs, with my fellow creatures, and, I know it
is yours. But, as all our SAVIOUR's matters, as to
outward form, now, are in a kind of confufion; each
muft be perfuaded, in his own mind, of his own circle,
and work; and ftand firm to his poft, till we more
clearly fee, our great SAVIOUR's meaning, in all his
various forms, and appearances, or meet above, where
we fhall fing one fong (and but one) and that moft
loudly, *Worthy is the* LAMB. I am, with a heart
full of cries, that your bow, may ever abide in ftrength,

Your moft obedient humble Servant,

H. H.

LETTER LV.
To the Rev. Mr Cooper, Kent.

Trevecka, Nov. 30th, 1768.

Dear Sir,

BEing not at home, when yours came, I hope you will excuse, my not answering it sooner, and especially, as I write but little—The hope of the LORD using you, to awaken, if it were but one soul, to feel the need of a SAVIOUR, and his righteousness, is, I doubt not, sufficient, to make you rejoice, in any cross, that he has appointed, for you to take up in his work. It is an infinite honour indeed to be employed by him, who made the Martyrs, and all that knew him truly, by his own Spirit, to rejoice in being counted worthy, to suffer for him. O dear Sir, did we but really believe, what we seem to believe, our hearts would be ever, in a flame of zeal for his cause, and our eyes would ever run with tears of real grief, that he is so neglected, and slighted, and the world so beloved, &c. And all, comparatively, venturing their souls to all eternity, on that original lie of the devil, " You shall not surely die " Sure we sleep, or else, pity to souls, that are round about us without GOD, in the world, would at least, make us spend much more of our time, in earnest prayer for them, with strong cries, and tears, to him who is able to save. How little do we see in reality, of the dreadful evil, of sin, the original universal fountain, that defiles our whole man, soul, body and spirit?

How

How little are we convinced, that we are enemies, to our SAVIOUR, and crucify him continually; and that it is infinite grace and patience, that we are not lifting up our eyes in torments? O Grace, grace! why are we not like all others, yielding all willing obedience to our lusts, and to the father of them, the god of this world, the devil? Surely, the cry of our grateful hearts must be, why me LORD, why me? who made thee to differ? O may you all, and all the young men, that are thrust out into the Vineyard, to testify of a dying Redeemer, and to awaken a fallen, dead Church and nation, have all the spirit's armour, and go forth indeed in the name of the LORD, from conquering, to conquer: having sat down, to cast up the cost, and be means of snatching thousands of perishing souls, out of the darkness, and chains of nature, and tyranny of sin, and Satan. This is, and by grace, shall be, ever the real cry of, dear Sir,

Yours, most affectionately, in the

Bonds of the Gospel, whilst

H. H.

LETTER LVI.

To Capt. Wilson.

Trevecka, Dec. 31st, 1769.

Dear Sir,

I Trust, that the glory of our SAVIOUR's kingdom, and of all his matters, shines stronger daily, on your soul; and if he is GOD himself, how great, how important are all the concerns of his house?

How

How really high indeed, the dignity of the meaneſt offices there? but who believes this? All the knowledge, of that moſt glorious object, is almoſt doctrinal only, and confequently, rather imaginary, than real, hence the coldneſs of love to him, and each other, and our indifference, about fpreading the knowledge of him, and bringing our fellow creatures to him proceeds. *The Son of Man when he comes, ſhall he find faith on the earth?* Let us bleſs him for what we know, fee, and feel; and fee it, as it really is, the higheſt honor, to do any thing, yea the leaſt, and meaneſt fervice, in his houſe. O let this holy, and humble ambition, ever enflame our hearts, and be never extinguiſhed. O my dear Sir, all feek themfelves, and go after him by halves, loving him but little, and ourfelves very much, none but himfelf, could bear with fuch fervants, and fuch fervice. O the veil that hides him, and all his glory; what patience muſt he have, with fuch ſtupid, wilful, blind, and ungrateful creatures, as we are? How amazing, that notwithſtanding all we have received, we ſhould not be more fruitful, and thankful to him, for all things? Yet, for all this, are we in hope, of being made a part of his glorious train above, to behold his glory, and be for ever with him? Then, whilſt we have a being, let our cry be, *Worthy is the* LAMB; waiting, in a lively hope, to behold his glory, and of being like him, and with him for ever. What a fweet cordial is the witneſs of the Holy Spirit, that GOD is our Father, and Redeemer; that all our care, friends and foes, are his. O, my

dear

dear Sir, it is time to awake: I truft, you do, put h'm in mind about me, that, as I have fo much, continually pardoned, and am indeed fo much beloved; I may alfo love much, and that my laft work, may be greater than my firft. May you, and your dear Sifter, ever find him prefiding over you, and making his abode with you, revealing himfelf, in all his characters, and relations, to your precious fouls. And may he ever be your principal topic, of hearing, and converfation. May the myftery, meaning, and application, of our SAVIOUR's circumcifion be opened to us, and may we enter on the new year, with circumcifed hearts. *Amen* and *Amen*.

I am, dear Captain, with all cordial
    regards to yourfelf, and Sifter,
        moft affectionately, in our dear Redeemer,
            H. H.

LETTER LVII.
To a young Minifter.

Trevecka, April 7th, 1771.

Dear Mr. E——,

I Have been at *Bath*, &c. for fome time, and am but lately returned, otherwife, I fhould have anfwered yours fooner. I truft, that every truth, finks deeper daily into your fpirit, fo as to bias your very nature. As a fpirit of thoughtleffnefs, yea, difinclination fills the dead, unawakened world, and I am afraid, too much influences, ferious people and fuch as are in fome meafure roufed up, to hear the truth.

I never

I never faw more need, of diftinguifhing, the common illumination, drawings, and convictions of the Holy Spirit, that not only may, but if it goes no farther, certainly will come to nothing: from the real faving faith, that truly unites our fouls, and fpirits, to the dear Redeemer, for ever, with an indiffoluble tie. This purifies the heart, and goes ftrait forward, thro' life, and death, to its own object; looking not at the prefent, but future reward. Doth truly, and internally feed on the Redeemer, and does as really live on the dear SAVIOUR, as by nature we lived to felf, and our own wills, and praife. My dear friend, if our SAVIOUR fends you out, as he did his firft Minifters, you muft expect to meet oppofition, from *Jews*, and *Greeks*, as they did. But, as he ftood by them, to carry them thro' all oppofition, he is ftill the fame, willing, and able, to carry you through. I have trufted him alone, for above thirty-fix years, and find him faithfully anfwer, and fulfil, all the offices, names, and characters, he affumes in his word. And have found, and do find, more than ever, all that is faid of vile Apoftates, fallen men, to be true, fo it is clear to me, who am the chief of all finners, and the leaft in GOD's houfe; and it is eafy for me to cry, LORD, I am as a brute beaft before thee, and to efteem others better than my felf. I had many fweet moments with dear Mr. *Fletcher*, at *Bath*, whom the LORD is much with; and I hope, he will leave great bleffings behind him. O may the Redeemer carry on his work with power, thro' a faithful, heart-fearch-ing miniftry, by fending faithful Labourers into his harveft, and qualify fuch witneffes, as fhall fhake, and awaken the poor world, and even profeffors alfo, from their fleepy, carnal, unbelieving condition. May fuch a foundation be laid, as the gates of hell fhall not be able to prevail againft it, that faith propagated that removes all mountains of difficulties, which feem to be in the way, and fet up the dear Saviour of finners, on the throne of the heart, in all his offices. This, and this alone, will ftand the fire, and teft of the laft day. O may the heart-felt knowledge of a dying God, be fpread far and near! and may the true Apoftolic faith, and primitive, univerfal love, fimplicity, and devotednefs to him, fill the land, yea, fill the whole earth. *Amen.*

So prays, Dear, Mr. F———,

Yours moft fincerely, in all

the various Parts of Chriftianity,

H. H.

F I N I S.

on his work with power, thro' a faithful, heart-search-ing miniſtry, by ſending faithful Labourers into his harveſt, and qualify ſuch witneſſes, as ſhall ſhake, and awaken the poor world, and even profeſſors alſo, from their ſleepy, carnal, unbelieving condition. May ſuch a foundation be laid, as the gates of hell ſhall not be able to prevail againſt it, that faith propagated that removes all mountains of difficulties, which ſeem to be in the way, and ſet up the dear SAVIOUR of ſinners, on the throne of the heart, in all his offices. This, and this alone, will ſtand the fire, and teſt of the laſt day. O may the heart-felt knowledge of a dying GOD, be ſpread far and near ! and may the true Apoſtolic faith, and primitive, univerſal love, ſimplicity, and devotedneſs to him, fill the land, yea, fill the whole earth. *Amen.*

So prays, Dear, Mr. F————,
Yours moſt ſincerely, in all
the various Parts of Chriſtianity,
H. H.

F I N I S.

CPSIA information can be obtained at www.ICGtesting.com
Printed in the USA
243712LV00003B/252/P